D1606026

WORLDMASK

WORLD

MASK

AKIVA TATZ

TARGUM/FELDHEIM

First published 1995

Printing plates by Frank, Jerusalem

Published by:
Targum Press Inc.
22700 W. Eleven Mile Rd.
Southfield, Mich. 48034

in conjunction with
Mishnas Rishonim

Distributed by:
Feldheim Publishers
200 Airport Executive Park
Nanuet, N.Y. 10954

Distributed in Israel by:
Targum Press Ltd.
POB 43170
Jerusalem 91430

Printed in Israel

בֵּית מִדְרָשׁ לְמוֹרוֹת

BETH MIDRASH LEMOROTH

Founded by: Mr A. KOHN

Principal: Rabbi M. MILLER

50, BEWICK ROAD
GATESHEAD NE8 4DQ
Telephone: 091-477 2620
091-477 1566

ב״ה

Tishri 5756

It is gratifying to know that the forebodings embodied in my letter of approbation to the previous work of Rabbi Akiva Tatz, *Living Inspired,* were completely unfounded. There I wrote "It is a work of profundity and inspiration and one wonders whether the modern frenetic westernized world is attuned to such depth of thought." It has been brought to my attention that the book quickly became a best seller – my apologies to the modern westernized world!

In his present work, *Worldmask,* Rabbi Tatz has scaled new heights in elucidating philosophical problems relating to our Emunah with his typical clarity and sensitivity, based entirely on classical Torah sources.

The problems dealt with are not merely theoretical but are relevant to central life issues.

The reader who pays careful attention to the clarifications embodied in this work will surely feel enlightened and uplifted.

This is another masterpiece which deserves wholehearted recommendation to every serious student of Torah thought.

Mi Miller

Rabbi M. Miller

קבלנו מרבותינו כי אחר שהותרה כתיבת תושבע"פ משום "עת
לעשות לה"" וגו' אין זה היתר בלבד, אלא שאף הכתיבה נעשתה אופן
של מסירה והעתקה של תושבע"פ ואפשר לטעום טעם של "מפי
השמועה" אף מפי הכתב, והנה ידידי הנעלה הרב מו"ה עקיבא ד"ר טץ
שליט"א שהוא אחד מגדולי מקדשי שם שמים כיום בחן שהוצק
בשפתותיו ובכוחו לקרב רחוקים ולהראות להם את יפי' ונשגבותה
של תורה כבר איתמחי גברא בספריו הקודמים לצקת בהם את כח
הדיבור פה אל פה להיות מזריע זרע ועושה פרי בלב השומעים
והקוראים, ועתה בספרו זה הרי הוא מוסיף והולך ומעלה בקדש,
וברכתי לרהמ"ח שליט"א שהנו שתול בבית ה', שיתקיים בו בחצרות
אלקינו יפריחו ויעשה פירות הילולים בלב מקבלי דבריו כי המעין
שהוא שואב ממנו מבית ה' הוא יוצא, יתן ה' וישארו המים חיים בכל
מקום שלשם יגיעו, וישמעו רחוקים ויבואו ויתנו לך כתר מלוכה
אכי"ר

בברכה

אלו שפי|רו

משה שפירא

Letter of Approbation from Rabbi Moshe Shapira שליט"א

בס'ד

Acknowledgments

Apart from sources quoted directly in the text, almost everything in this book is derived from the words of Rabbi Moshe Shapira שליט׳א, and Rabbi Mordechai Miller שליט׳א; much of it derives originally from Rabbi Dessler זצ׳ל.

The following people provided essential assistance and I thank them:

* My mother, Mrs. Minde Tatz, for her customary expert work on the manuscript;
* Tzodick and Gillian Merkel for their gracious support;
* The staff of Targum Press for exceptional courtesy, efficiency and patience;
* My wife, Suzanne, who makes it that much easier to see through the world's mask.

A.T.
Cheshvan 5756
November 1995

Contents

Introduction

This world is a mask which hides a higher world. But it is a unique mask: it hides, and yet it reveals. It is opaque and yet transparent. The face behind the mask hides or shines through, depending on the viewer.

Just as a human face is only an outer layer and yet is able to reveal that which is within by its movements and nuances of expression, so too the world reveals its depth to the one who studies it carefully. The very word for face, *panim*, has two root meanings which reflect these opposites: *panim*, face, and *p'nim*, internality. That which is only the outer face is also that which most closely reflects the inner depth.

We have no direct access to the depth; we see only the face. The spiritual path requires learning the skill of reading the signs in the outer dimension in order to perceive the inner world. Just as we discover the personality and soul of another human being by carefully observing the shades of expression reflected in that person's body and face, we must train ourselves to read that face of reality which is the physical world in order to discover its personality and soul.

This book traces some of the Torah themes which reflect this duality, both within the world and beyond it, in physical expression and in root depth. The careful reader who explores the chapters presented here, in their sequence, will discover some of the keys which unlock the world behind the mask.

Chapter 1

Torah - the Cause of Reality

Torah and the world parallel each other exactly. Torah is the spiritual core, the world is its physical expression. Although this idea is quite well-known, at its heart is an element which is often entirely unknown or seriously misunderstood. Let us delve into the relationship between Torah and the world as deeply as possible in order to discover some of the true wonder which it contains.

The nature of the parallel between Torah and physical reality is that *Torah is the cause and the world is the result.* It is not enough to understand that there is a correspondence between every detail of the physical universe and the Torah; it is essential to realize that each detail of the world exists *because the Torah says so.* In fact, every fine nuance of each detail exists exactly as it does in the world only because the Torah itself contains each of those details within details.

The analogy most commonly used to portray this relationship is that of a blueprint – the Torah is the blueprint of the world; just as an architect first draws up plans and the builder then follows those plans when building the physical structure, Hashem first brought the Torah into being and then created the world using the Torah as its plan: *"Istakel b'Oraisa u'bara alma* – He looked into the Torah and created the world." But there is another depth here: the Torah is not simply a plan in the sense of an architect's drawings; it is a plan in the sense of *genes* which themselves actually *carry out the construction* of the organism which results from the code carried in those genes. Certainly, the genetic code corresponds to the physical features which the organism possesses, but it would be a serious mistake to imagine that this correspondence is *descriptive*, that the genes somehow reflect in coded form the physical reality; the genes do not describe, they do not reflect – they are the *reason* that the body looks as it does, they are the instructions and the mechanism which construct the physical. In fact, the body is a reflection of the genes!

The Torah is the genetic material of the world. The words of Torah are Hashem's words; but Hashem's word was not simply spoken by Him at the time of the Creation (and then recorded in the Torah later) while He created the world by some unrelated means; His word *was the means, the mechanism of Creation*. Each word spoken by Hashem in creating the world crystallized into the object it described; this is the secret of the two meanings of the word *"davar"* – an "object", and a "word"; an object in the world *is* Hashem's word concretized.

But there is more. The Torah is not simply a record of the Creation and a history of the world; the Nefesh Hachaim explains that the Creation is ongoing, the Universe is constantly being brought into being by the Creator each instant just as at the first instant. Hashem's word is continuously spoken, and it is continuously condensing into the matter and events of the world. *And since the Torah is Hashem's word, the Torah is the medium of Creation always.* Not a history, not a description, but a cosmic mechanism bringing reality into being; the genes of the world.

*   *   *

This idea is particularly difficult to grasp in the modern era. Western thought is firmly based in the finite, physical dimensions; the yardstick of reality is the laboratory, and that which is not tangible or measurable by experiment is not taken seriously. The entire world of spirituality is relegated to the domain of personal experience and personal belief. The classical Western mind does not engage transcendence. At center stage in this grasp of the world is the fact of physical existence; spiritual wisdom is seen, at best, as commentary.

The result of this worldview when applied to Torah is the notion that Torah describes, analyses, comments. One often hears admiring statements about Torah flowing from this perspective – how deep the Torah is, how penetratingly it perceives the almost imperceptible shades of all aspects of the world. But in reality this is nonsense and one who speaks thus speaks against Torah.

To make this point clearer, let us consider a typical example. One often hears it said that the idea behind the laws of *kashrus* (permitted and forbidden foods) is health – certain foods are not kosher because they are unhealthy. The Torah, in its great wisdom, prohibits such foods in order to safeguard the health of those who heed its commands. Some types of meat are prone to tapeworm infestation; shellfish inhabit parts of the seabed which are contaminated with hepatitis virus and other pathogens, and so on.

Of course there is truth in this approach – Torah living *is* healthy; a major benefit of the Torah-observant way of life is in fact the physical and mental well-being which is an integral element of Torah observance. But a moment's thought will show the fundamental error of this point of view: *such a person understands the physical world to be primary*, the world is the way it is as a primary fact – some foods are unhealthy, some are not; that is simply the way things are. And now, *after the fact*, the Torah deals with that reality: eat this food, do not eat that. The Torah is secondary to a finite world, and of course it too must be finite. The absolutely inevitable next step is: of course, the Torah must be subject to change! Previously unkosher foods which are no longer unhealthy due to modern inventions or improvements can now be eaten! After all, the entire basis for the prohibition was a health consideration!

But the spiritual secret is quite the opposite. Certain foods are forbidden; the reason is *entirely spiritual*, whether we grasp some of that spiritual depth or not. The *primary* element is the spiritual, the transcendent. In fact, it could be that the physical attributes of the forbidden food are as they are *because* the spiritual essence is impure: the shellfish inhabits its contaminated habitat and may be physically unhealthy *because it is unkosher!*

This is the grasp which a Jew should have. An effort must be made to break the patterns of Western thought which bind the world within finite boundaries if one wishes to become spiritually conscious. Transcendent wisdom must be primary.

The secularized modern view breaks all of Torah into fragments of finite proportion. Shabbos is perceived as a day of rest in the sense of physical rest; its prohibitions are those of work in the sense of physical exertion. And of course, we can do as we please with those prohibitions because times have changed – what was work in earlier times is no longer work! Lighting a fire was once a tiring procedure and that is why it was forbidden; today it is done with a flick of the wrist and so it must be permitted!

And again, the truth is entirely different. The observance of Shabbos is a *spiritual* matter; the idea of physical rest is very much secondary. In fact, there is no Torah prohibition of physical exertion at all. Lighting a flame is a creative act and that is the essential element, the degree of physical exertion is *irrelevant.* And lighting a flame today is every bit as creative as it ever was. But secular eyes see a finite world, and refracted through that prism all of spirituality is reduced to the dimensions of a very limited human angle of vision.

*   *   *

Armed with the knowledge that Torah is primary, we must now ask: "Where is Torah?" Is the primary, causal Torah that we have been discussing a parchment scroll and no more? What *exactly* do we mean when we speak of Torah as the primary energy of the world?

The answer is that Torah is located in the Oral Law, the *Torah she'b'al peh.* The Torah lives and makes contact with the world in the Oral Law. *And the Oral Law lives only in the hearts and minds of the Sages of the Jewish people and of all those who learn it.* To the extent that Torah is studied, it lives in the world; if it is neglected, it is not here.

When the king Yannai was considering killing the Sages of his generation, he asked his advisor "If I destroy the Sages, what will be the future of Torah – *Torah mai t'he aleha?"* The answer was "It is rolled and rests in a corner; let all who wish to study it come and study." Yannai satisfied himself with that reply and proceeded with his plan. But the *gemara* states: That is true of the Written Law, (that it is accessible to all in the form of a written scroll), but Yannai should have asked *"What about the Oral Law?"*

The Oral Law is not contained in written words. No scroll or book can hold it. It is inscribed in the consciousness of the one who labors to understand it, and in that consciousness only. (This idea itself is accessible only to one who has experienced it; no amount of explanation can convey the organic, dynamic experience of the blossoming of understanding on multiple levels which is the reward of exertion in Torah study.)

And now we can open a startling new awareness: if Torah lives in the minds and personalities of its Sages, *that is where the causative, primary energy of the world is to be found.* This most profound idea means that Hashem's Torah *is* the consciousness of the Sages of *Torah she'b'al peh.* It has been given to us; it is no longer in Heaven, so to speak, and we are partners in Creation in the deepest sense possible.

The *gemara* itself teaches this principle. In a debate about a particular point of practical *halacha* (Torah law) Rabbi Yehoshua and a majority of the Sages present held a particular opinion. Rabbi Eliezer held differently. But Rabbi Eliezer refused to accept the majority opinion despite the principle that we follow the majority, because he held that if the minority opinion is patently and provably correct it is superior to the majority! And of course one cannot vote on that issue either!

So Rabbi Eliezer proceeded to bring proof that his opinion was the correct one. Very compelling proof, in fact: he stated that if his opinion were correct, a carob tree which was nearby should provide proof. And that is what happened – in full view of the assembled Sages, the carob tree uprooted itself and moved. But the Sages answered simply "We do not bring proof from a carob tree."

The depth here is that Rabbi Eliezer was of course not trying to impress anyone with his personal greatness; he was simply bringing outside, objective proof for his opinion since he had to contend with a majority opinion which opposed his, and the only way to demonstrate his correctness was with proof outside of human reasoning.

The *gemara* continues: Rabbi Eliezer stated that a stream flowing by should prove him correct. The water in the stream reversed and flowed uphill. The reply? "We do not bring proof from streams of water."

Rabbi Eliezer then declared that the walls of the *beis midrash* (study hall) should prove his opinion true. In deference to him the walls began to collapse, but in deference to Rabbi Yehoshua their collapse was arrested and they hung suspended.

Rabbi Eliezer made one last attempt to prove his point. "Let it be proved from Heaven that I am correct," he said. And a Heavenly voice was heard. We can only begin to picture the scene: a carob tree moving around outside, a stream of water flowing uphill, the Sages seated under walls somehow suspended, and a Divine voice is heard. The *gemara* records that the voice stated *"Halacha k'moso b'kol makom!"* – The law is as Rabbi Eliezer holds *in all cases!*

In the silence that followed Rabbi Yehoshua arose and said: *"Lo ba'shamayim hi* – It (the Torah) is not in Heaven.*"* Heavenly voices notwithstanding, a vote was taken and the *halacha* was decided according to the majority and against Rabbi Eliezer. *The Torah is not in Heaven;* it has been given into our dominion.

The *gemara* goes on to state something even more amazing than the foregoing, if that is possible to imagine. One of the Sages subsequently saw *Eliyahu ha'Navi* – Elijah the Prophet. He took the opportunity to ask Elijah: "At that time (when that vote was taken), what was Hashem doing?" And Elijah answered "He was smiling and saying *'Nitzchuni banai, nitzchuni banai* – My children have defeated Me, My children have defeated Me!'"

The *gemara* does not quote amazing incidents for their novelty. All *divrei Torah,* words of Torah, contain essential lessons. What is being taught here is the principle that the Torah, that same Torah which is the agency of Creation, lives in the hearts of the Sages of the Oral Law. Hashem Himself, as it were, agrees with their rulings *because He has entrusted them with His Torah,* He has given it into the human realm. *Lo ba'shamayim hi.*

And that is why, by applying Torah law, (in this case the law of majority), we bring reality into being, and the result becomes Divinely true! And a sensitive ear will hear that this, too, is the very reason that Rabbi Eliezer can exert dominion over physical reality; the objects and phenomena of the world bend to his will, shape themselves *according to his Torah.*

* * *

There is a well-known passage in the Talmud Yerushalmi stating that physical changes occur in the human body as the result of a *halachic* ruling of the Sages, and the understanding that the world shapes itself according to the Torah of the Sages is the key to many seemingly unfathomable sections of *gemara*. Let us examine an example in order to feel this.

The *gemara* records the case of a certain Reb Nechunia *"chofer shichin"* – digger of wells. His particular merit was that he dug wells in order to provide water for travellers. It once happened that his daughter fell into a well and was unable to get out. (There is an opinion that the well into which she fell was in fact one of those that her father had dug.) It was impossible to extricate her, and it seemed inevitable that she would drown; in those particular circumstances a person could survive for no longer than three hours.

The leading Sage of that generation was Rabbi Chanina ben Dosa, and the people came to him with the report of Reb Nechunia's daughter. At the end of the first hour he said "Shalom"; implying that all would be well. After a second hour he again said "Shalom." At the end of the third hour, when it had become impossible for her to survive in the water any longer, he said *"Alsa* – She has emerged."

Rabbi Chanina was correct – the girl had in fact emerged from the well; upon questioning her it transpired that she had been saved in a seemingly miraculous manner. Wondering how Rabbi Chanina had known that she would be saved, the people asked him "Are you a prophet?" Rabbi Chanina answered "I am no prophet and I am not the son of a prophet. But should a man's child suffer harm in an area in which he labored?" In other words, Rabbi Chanina was saying that if Reb Nechunia had the merit of providing water for the Jewish people, it could not happen that a child of his should come to harm through water.

The *gemara* goes on to state: "Despite this, his son died of thirst." Reb Nechunia had a son who perished from thirst after the incident described previously in which his daughter was saved. The *gemara* explains that Reb Nechunia suffered this loss because "Around Him it is very stormy," meaning that people of greatness are judged by the most exacting standards. Those close to Hashem are held to a hairsbreadth; Reb Nechunia may have possessed great merit, but due to his greatness, his merit was not sufficient to ensure salvation for his son.

At this point an obvious question arises: if Reb Nechunia's merit was not sufficient to save his son, how did it save his daughter previously? And on the other hand, if it was sufficient to save her, why did it not suffice for his son?

This question is asked by the *Shita Mekubetzes*, and the cryptic answer given in the name of Rabbi Yechiel is: "That *tzaddik* was no longer alive." What does this mean?

The meaning is this: at the time when Reb Nechunia's daughter was in danger, Rabbi Chanina was alive; when Reb Nechunia's son was in danger, however, Rabbi Chanina was no longer alive. How does this information answer our question? The answer is that while Rabbi Chanina lives to say that a man cannot be harmed in an area in which he has exerted himself in exemplary fashion, that is the case – such a person cannot be harmed, and the reason is *because Rabbi Chanina says so!* There is no intrinsic rule in the Torah or the world which mandates that Reb Nechunia's children will be protected by his merit; that reality comes into being when a

Torah sage of Rabbi Chanina's caliber reasons that it should be so. His mind is Torah, his reasoning is Torah, his opinion is Torah. And if it is Torah, it is causative in the world; the world must shape itself accordingly.

But when Rabbi Chanina is no longer alive, when he is no longer present to hold an opinion on the workings of Providence, the world reverts to its usual form; things operate according to their usual pattern. While a Torah Sage holds an opinion, Hashem Himself defers to that opinion, as it were. When that Sage no longer lives to hold his Torah opinion, Hashem enforces His own opinion once again!

* * *

The idea that the words of the Oral Law hold creative energy holds true even when those words are subject to argument. Even when the opinion of a Torah Sage is opposed by that of another Torah authority, and even when the two opinions would seem to be mutually exclusive, they are both true. The depth of this concept and its derivation in Torah require separate discussion, but let us at least make mention of an example and take note of its practical outcome.

An incident is quoted in the name of the Chazon Ish. A man approached the Chazon Ish for advice concerning a difficult medical problem. He had a growth in his lung which seemed incurable and potentially lethal, and his doctors in Israel had suggested that he travel to Europe where some hope of a cure might exist. In Israel at the time they had nothing to offer in the way of effective treatment, and the man asked the Chazon Ish what he should do.

The Chazon Ish told the man to remain in Israel. He did so, and recovered. When asked what had prompted his advice to the patient not to leave the land of Israel, the Chazon Ish answered that he had simply looked up the matter in the Code of Jewish Law. He explained as follows: "When that man described his lung problem to me, I recognized it as being the same as a particular problem which occurs in the lungs of animals. We know that certain medical problems of animals are comparable to those of humans, and this particular lung problem is discussed in the *gemara* and the Shulchan Aruch, the Code of Jewish Law.

"In the Shulchan Aruch there is a difference of opinion concerning the status of an animal which has such a lesion. The author of the Shulchan Aruch, Rabbi Yosef Karo, holds that it is kosher. The Rama, the great European authority whose opinion is definitive for Ashkenazi Jewry, holds that it is *treif*, forbidden. Now when we say that an animal is kosher despite having some abnormality of an internal organ, we mean that the particular abnormality in question is not lethal. Such an animal could live normally; its life is not immediately endangered by the abnormality. However, an animal that is *treif* is by definition a dying animal; its anatomical abnormality is lethal within months – this is the very thing which renders it unkosher.

"So when the author of the Shulchan Aruch holds that this type of animal is kosher, he is saying, in effect, that he holds that this type of lung problem is not lethal. The Rama, on the other hand, who holds that the animal is *treif*, must hold that the problem *is* lethal. Now these two great Torah authorities are the definitive *halachic* opinions in two different jurisdictions, in a sense – the author of the Shulchan Aruch is considered the *moreh d'asra*, the local authority, in the Land of Israel, whereas the Rama is the definitive authority in Europe.

"I explained to the man that these great Torah opinions are not simply assessments or descriptions of reality; they are *causative*. If the Shulchan Aruch holds that such an animal can live despite its problem, *such an animal can live*. And if the Rama holds that this animal will die as a result of its problem, *the animal will die*. Therefore in Europe, where the world is formed by the Torah of the Rama, *this type of lung disease is lethal*; if you go there you will be in great danger. But here in *Eretz Yisrael*, where reality takes shape according to the opinions of the Shulchan Aruch, *this same problem is not dangerous*, and therefore you had better stay put!"

Chapter 2

The Mask of Nature

I. THE MASK

We can gain access to the spiritual world only through the mask of the physical. The world of nature hides the spiritual; it does this by appearing to be self-sufficient, running reliably along the same track with reassuring predictability. The difference between nature and miracle is that the miraculous breaks the expected pattern.

Intrinsically, however, a miracle is no more wonderful than the natural – there is an allusion to this at the splitting of the sea: when the Jewish people had crossed over, Moshe was commanded to stretch out his staff over the sea to bring the waters back to their original natural position. The question which presents itself is: why was an act necessary for this? To split the sea an act was necessary because that was miraculous; nature had to be set aside. But surely, as soon as the Jewish people were safe and the need for the miracle was over, nature should have re-asserted itself automatically – there is a principle that the world resists miracles as much as possible (for reasons which should become clear as we study this subject further.) The departure from normality requires a special act, but why does return to normality do so too? The answer is that *nature is miraculous* no less than its rarest exceptions. For the sea to manifest in the way that we are used to seeing it is no less the express wish and manifestation of the Creator than the once-in-history splitting of that sea. The only difference is that we are used to the one and the other is unexpected.

We are lulled into insensitivity by the routine of nature; we take for granted that with which we are familiar. The Hebrew word for nature is *teva*, the root of which means "to drown"; if the world of natural cause and effect is not carefully and perceptively studied for its clues to depth, it drowns awareness of the spiritual. But the word *teva* is also the root of *matbe'a*, meaning a coin which has an embossed image stamped on its surface: the world is a stamped-out image of a higher reality. If one studies the world with the knowledge that it accurately reflects its source, one can perceive the features of that source surely and consistently. The choice is entirely the observer's – one can look at the world with the tired eyes of habit and see only the mechanical, only that which drowns the spirit; or one can look with eyes of wonder and see the image of a higher reality.

*   *   *

II. PERCEPTION

Among those who walk the spiritual path there are varying levels of perception. We can define four general levels of relationship with the physical world. (It may be a humbling experience to attempt to identify one's own personal level as we move through this discussion.)

An individual at the first (and lowest) of these four levels relates to the world in the following way. This person is clearly aware of Hashem's existence (note that this is the minimal level!) In fact, he *davens* (prays) intensely. But his understanding of the world is that it exists as an entity separate from Hashem. To be sure, Hashem created the world and controls it; He can override the natural cause-and-effect of the laws of nature; but if He does not specifically override nature, nature proceeds on its own. When this person prays, his prayer is usually phrased as "Let it be..."; for example: "Hashem, I need to be at a certain place at a certain time, and I know that many things could prevent my being there – after all, I cannot control all the variables that must coincide in order for me to be there then; therefore, Hashem, please *let it happen*."

In this person's mind, the world functions according to its laws and most planned events have a reasonable chance of occurring; only, there is no guarantee that this particular event will occur because all sorts of things could get in the way – bad weather, illness, failure of mechanical equipment at a critical time, in fact any number of unpredictable and uncontrollable factors could confound his plan. He feels that his goal is attainable only if Hashem "lets it be", that is, if He does not actively prevent it. What this person *really means* in his prayer is "Hashem, please don't interfere!" The natural world will take its predictable course as long as there is no Divine interference.

The problem with this view of the world is that it sees Hashem as being *outside of nature*. In control, of course; supreme, of course; but outside and separate nevertheless. If nature has an existence outside of Hashem's existence, then the fundamental principle of the all-encompassing Oneness of the Divine is lacking. The person on this level is trapped in a false perception of the world; he has accepted the routine of nature as evidence that it is self-sufficient and solid. Nature, *teva*, has drowned him.

When a person on this level says *"Shma Yisrael..."* he usually understands that this declaration of Hashem's Oneness means that there is only one Divine Being. Of course he is correct, but there is a lot more to the *"Shma"* than that. The idea of *"Hashem Echad* – Hashem is One" is not only to exclude two or more; it does not only mean that there is no other god besides Hashem; *it means that there is nothing else at all.* When one says the word *"Echad* – One" the idea which should be brought into focus is *"Ein od milvado* – There is nothing other than Him"; no world, no nature; in fact in the meditation of that moment even the consciousness of one's own existence melts into the Divine Oneness. This can be a very powerful and perhaps unsettling experience; for this and other reasons we do not prolong this thought excessively – an untrained mind may forget to return to the world of obligation and action! The work here is to remember *"Ein od milvado"* always and yet to function within the world fully.

*　　*　　*

The second level is more advanced. One who has attained the second level is fully aware that there is nothing separate from Hashem. Every leaf that falls, every atom that vibrates is a direct manifestation of Hashem's control. There is no object or phenomenon in the world which exists or moves independently. The person who sees the world thus conceives of nature as a tool in the hand of the Creator – the tool moves only as the hand moves, no more and no less.

This level far surpasses the first; the question, however, is what is wrong with this view of nature? Surely one whose consciousness constantly grasps the natural as nothing other than immediately and directly controlled by the Creator has reached a high level of spiritual awareness?

The fault here is much more subtle than that of the first level, but it is a fault nonetheless. The problem with the view of nature as a tool in the hand of Hashem is as follows. *A tool always implies a deficiency.* A tool is always used where the user cannot act without it. Even where the user himself has invented and manufactured the tool, he has done so only because he is unable to perform the function of that tool unaided.

One or two illustrations of this principle will clarify it. There is a very simple tool which some people use when taking a bath – it consists of a sponge attached to the end of a bar which is about the length of one's arm. This device is used for washing one's back. Anyone who has used such a device will agree that it is highly effective; but the point to understand here is that one uses this object *only because one cannot reach one's back without it.* No-one uses this tool for washing the abdomen! A tool is an extension of the user where the user cannot reach or function without that tool. This is an invariable rule in the use of tools.

Another example will illustrate further. If one runs a business, let us say a shop, which expands its clientele until one is forced to take on an assistant, the same principle will be seen to operate. The business has grown until one can no longer manage alone. The hiring of the assistant is a symptom of the fact that one is limited – if one could manage perfectly well alone that assistant would not have been hired. Again, we see that any extension of the self that is external to the self is a sure sign of limitation.

If this rule is true of tools in general, and we say that nature is a tool in the Creator's hand, we are implying that He somehow needs that tool; surely, if He were able to manifest as He wishes without any tool He would do so directly. If nature is a tool we would have to say that whatever it is that Hashem wants to achieve by means of His Creation, He chooses to achieve through the creation and manipulation of nature. Of course, He is the inventor and manufacturer of this tool, but the question remains – why would He use a tool if He could do the job Himself, as it were? So the person on this level, while not falling into the error of seeing nature as *independent* from Hashem, nevertheless does see nature as *other than* Hashem in the sense of a tool in the hand of an artisan, with the deficiency inherent in this view.

*   *   *

The third level is the domain of those whose perception of Hashem's all-encompassing Oneness is clear. At this level there is no distinction between Hashem and His Creation; the world of nature is not a tool or extension of the Creator – it is none other than Hashem Himself manifesting. This is the level of full consciousness of *"Ein od milvado –*

There is nothing other than Him." The perception of one who has reached this elevated plane has none of the deficiencies of the previous levels; here there is no dichotomy between Creator and Creation. At this level, no tools are necessary, no tools exist – every leaf that falls, every atom that vibrates is a direct manifestation of the Creator Himself.

The question that must be answered here is: how do people at this exalted level understand nature? After all, they see the natural world clearly; if in truth there is none other than the Creator's presence manifesting, why is there a world of nature? Why is there a world of natural-seeming cause-and-effect which certainly appears to be independent and self-maintaining? For what reason does the Creator set up a world which appears to hide Him?

The answer is precisely that: the world is designed to hide Him. And the most easily understood reason for that is in order to provide man with his most important possession: free will. In a world of seemingly independent cause-and-effect, of seemingly routine and predictable mechanical nature, one is not forced to perceive the Divine source. Of course, one may infer the presence of a Hand behind the scenes from the very mechanics and details of the natural, but one is not compelled to do so. Spiritual perception remains a voluntary exercise.

So the person on this third level understands that nature is a mask, a smokescreen. It exists in order to provide the freedom of choice which man must have in order to be human, and more than this – in order to resemble the Divine. And the ultimate purpose of the smokescreen is for man to penetrate it, to perceive that it is no more real than smoke.

*   *   *

The hallmark of one who has attained this level is the ability to perform miracles. Why is this so? Let us understand.

Rabbi Chanina ben Dosa found his daughter distressed because she had poured vinegar into the Shabbos lights instead of oil. Rabbi Chanina commented: "Let the One Who says that oil should burn say that vinegar should burn;" his daughter lit the vinegar – and it burned. "Let the One Who says that oil should burn..." – in other words, oil burns only because Hashem wills it to; it is a mistake to think that any intrinsic property of oil makes it combustible – it burns only because that is the will of its Creator. In truth, vinegar could burn just as easily – if that were the will of the Creator it would burn perfectly. Only the Creator has so set things up that He consistently wills oil to burn and not vinegar so that we perceive a natural process; we seek natural explanations and tend to conclude that things must be the way we perceive them.

But for one who does not see any natural process, for one who sees only the Divine Hand, *there is no need for the routine of nature to apply.* For Rabbi Chanina it makes no difference whether vinegar burns or not; just as oil burns only as a direct manifestation of the Creator's will, so too vinegar will burn if the Creator wills it. And Rabbi Chanina will not be surprised in the least. In fact, one who would register the faintest flicker of surprise at seeing vinegar burn is hopelessly distant from the level of spiritual attainment we are considering. And since it makes no difference to him, vinegar burns for him just as oil does.

An analogy will help to clarify this idea. Imagine that you are approached by a friend who is masked. From behind his mask, your friend challenges you to identify him and you struggle to perceive his identity. Let us say that eventually you realize exactly who it is. You correctly state your friend's name; his identity is revealed. What will your friend do at that point? The answer is that he will take off his mask; there is no point wearing a mask in front of one who sees through it. Masks and disguises are worn in order to prevent recognition of the one who wears them; once the wearer's identity is discovered the mask ceases to have any use.

And that is exactly the way that nature functions as a mask. Hashem wears nature like a mask; He hides behind it to give us the opportunity to exercise free will. But for the *tzaddik* who sees Hashem in everything, for that elevated individual who has penetrated the mask, *Hashem takes off the mask*. Nature is no longer serving to hide anything from such an individual, and therefore its constraints are unnecessary.

*   *   *

What wonders does the fourth level hold? How is it possible to be more elevated than the *tzaddikim* of former generations whom we have been studying? What extra dimension of perception is it possible to add for one who sees through the smokescreen surely and permanently?

The perception of the fourth level is really an added depth in the third. For the *tzaddik* at this rarefied and holy level, there is a problem; perhaps the correct term would be a certain suffering. There is a principle underlying all of Creation which expresses its true nature and purpose: *"Hakol bara lichvodo* – Everything is Created for His glory."

Everything in the Creation exists to bring out the honor and glory of the One who Creates it; all of the Creation is designed so that it will ultimately reveal the greatness of the Divine.

The problem is that the smokescreen, the mask of nature, seems to contradict this principle. In depth, the mask of nature which provides the opportunity for human freedom of choice will ultimately be perceived as a great element in the unfolding of Divine revelation. But now, while the Divine remains hidden by the world of nature, it seems as if nature works in opposition to the principle that all must reveal the Divine. Everything must declare the presence and glory of Hashem; a mask does the opposite. Despite the importance of human free will, nature is preventing the open and total revelation of the Divine which is the world's ultimate purpose.

For the *tzaddik* who sees this, nature is an indescribable creation. That Hashem should reveal Himself unhindered would be perfectly understandable. But that He should create that which hides Him, that which holds back His total and unlimited manifestation, is remarkable beyond description. The greatest wonder of all is the fact that there is a finite and natural world in the first place.

When a miracle occurs and the world sees clearly Who is in charge, such a *tzaddik* feels perfectly comfortable. But when nature manifests and Hashem's presence is hidden, he is uncomfortable. For this saintly individual, miracles are perfectly natural and nature is absolutely miraculous!

Chapter 3

Behind the Mask

So miracles reveal that nature is a mask. Behind that mask, there is none other than Hashem Himself. We must now ask: if all is from Hashem, if the entire world is a manifestation of His will, why should we act at all? Why is human effort necessary – would it not be better to acknowledge Hashem's mastery of the world by making no effort in the natural realm? And if our effort *is* required, how much is the proper amount? What is the purpose of our actions in the world, and how are we to handle the inevitable conflict between acknowledging Hashem's total mastery and our own apparent mastery of the natural?

This fundamental subject is best understood by appreciating that people at differing levels of spiritual development must relate to the question of human action *each according to his level*. And sometimes it is not the person but the situation which demands that the individual respond in a particular way to bring out the true nature of the relationship between natural and transcendent. Just as there are levels of perception of reality, as we have seen, so too there are levels of interaction with the natural – differing modes of handling the natural world and differing modes of interacting with the miraculous.

* * *

In this area of human activity we can discern five levels.

At the first and highest level are those for whom nature has no independent reality at all. These are the *tzaddikim* who have command over nature; as we have noted previously, since they see through the mask of nature, the mask is removed. Such people can perform miracles – we have noted the example of Rabbi Chanina ben Dosa for whom vinegar burns in place of oil because for him there is no difference between the burning of oil and the burning of vinegar – both are equally possible since each is a direct manifestation of the Creator's will. Human perception which is conditioned by the usual, the familiar, is irrelevant here. As we have noted, when open miracles occur in the presence of these *tzaddikim* they are unimpressed – or perhaps more accurately, they are just as impressed by nature as they are by miracle. They live within nature but transcend it. (Needless to say, in our generation such exalted individuals are extremely rare, if any exist at all. Our position in the long winding-down of *yeridas ha'doros* – the "descent of the generations" – leaves us far from any personal contact with such greatness.)

When we consider this highest of levels, a question arises. We find that when a miracle occurs for a *tzaddik*, it has a natural component; if the *tzaddik* initiates the miracle, it is always by performing an action within the natural. Why is this necessary? Why must these great individuals perform any natural effort at all? If miracles occur for them and the natural world does not constrain them, why must they act within the world?

A few examples will make the question clearer. When Noach is to be saved from the Flood, he is commanded to build an ark and take all species of animal on earth into it. But an ark of those dimensions could never hold all those animals! More than this: the Midrash states that the animals occupied only the middle of the three layers which the ark comprised – the upper level was for human habitation and the lower for waste. The entire event was miraculous. Now the question is: if the saving of the world's animal life was miraculous, why was a physical ark necessary at all? Why did Hashem not simply save all earthly life *without* commanding Noach to go through the motions, as it were, of building a vessel which was far too small for the purpose anyway?

We find Yaakov Avinu preparing to place a circle of stones around the spot where he is to sleep in order to ward off wild animals. But a few stones will not deter hungry predators! If Yaakov is relying on Hashem to protect him, why make a token effort in the natural?

Moshe Rabbenu is commanded to ascend the mountain in order to see the entire Land which he is forbidden to enter. But the entire Land of Israel is not visible from any one mountain! Again, why the effort if the result is to be miraculously out of proportion to that effort? Why does Hashem not simply show him the Land in a vision where he stands – the elevation of Mount Nevo is irrelevant anyway?

When Elisha revives the lad who has died he closes the door and proceeds to lie upon the boy, placing his eyes upon the boy's eyes, his mouth upon the boy's mouth, and so on. The lad revives miraculously. Why the procedure of lying upon him? And in this case we see that it was necessary even though no-one else was present – Scripture clearly states that Elisha closed the door; his actions were not meant for anyone else to perceive. If he is *davening* (praying) for Hashem to revive the child, and the result is clearly that his prayer is answered, why must he perform actions which are just as clearly inadequate in themselves?

We can find many more examples of this phenomenon. Rabbi Shimon bar Yochai is sustained in a cave for years by carobs and water. If Hashem is keeping him alive miraculously, why does He do so by miraculously providing carobs and water – why not simply sustain Rabbi Shimon without any food at all? Why does Rabbi Chanina ben Dosa give instructions to light the vinegar – why not simply produce flame with no material at all? When Elisha miraculously produces oil for the Shunamite woman, why does he start with a flask of oil which then miraculously fills all the empty vessels which are brought to it? Why not cause those vessels to be full of oil instantly and independently? In fact, why are the vessels needed in the first place – could they not also be produced miraculously together with their contents?

This matter is very deep, and it has many layers. The fact is that physical actions are the keys to the spiritual world. The Nefesh Hachaim explains in detail how changes in the higher worlds are brought about by our actions in this material world. Physical actions are *necessary* to produce changes in the non-physical; that is part of the secret of the very existence of the physical, and it is the reason that the human has been given a body. *We* cause the spiritual world to move. The physical world is like the keys of the piano – the music is not produced in the keys, it is produced in the strings hidden deep within the mechanism behind the facade; *but the keys are necessary.* Without those keys there is no access to the inner mechanism, and although the keys are dumb, when they are struck there is music.

Even when the result is out of all proportion to the magnitude of the physical action, there must be an action. When Pharaoh's daughter stretches out her arm to save the infant Moshe from the Nile although he is out of her reach, her arm miraculously elongates. Her effort, her attempt, is the key; when we make a sincere effort we may merit to see it amplified beyond expectation, but without some attempt there is nothing to amplify. We must act; if we are sufficiently spiritually developed we may be granted a view behind the mask to see that the result is really not dependent on the action at all. But act we must. We are never passive passengers.

There are further depths to this question, but let us select an approach along the lines of our discussion of varying spiritual levels. Some of the classical commentaries ask our question – why is any action necessary on the part of a *tzaddik* who knows that action is not the real cause of whatever results in the world, and who can perform supernatural feats at will? They answer as follows: the *tzaddik* performs an action in causing a miracle *in order to minimize the miracle* – his humility demands that there be at least some natural component of whatever transpires so that he remains bound to the physical world, as it were; he is constrained at least to some degree by the appearance of cause and effect. He is hiding the miracle from himself; or rather, he is hiding from the fact that his level is such that he wields control over the natural. Indeed, we find that Hashem commands such behavior – Moshe Rabbenu is instructed to climb the mountain in order to view the Land of Israel; Noach is ordered to build the ark. At this level, the action is a token. The *tzaddik* is prevented from soaring away from the natural even as he controls it; no degree of greatness ever transcends humility. In fact, it is just this quality of humility which has elevated the *tzaddik* to his level in the first place; exactly *because* he sees that he is empty of independent existence, *because* he sees that the natural is only a veil, *because* he has trained himself to perceive that he and the world are nothing and that Hashem is everything, because of this he is who he is. He resists doing anything which would appear to be the result of his own greatness.

*   *   *

At the second level are those people for whom nature and miracle are not quite one (or those whose work is to teach the correct handling of this level even though they themselves have transcended it). At this level miracles are possible, even commonplace, but those who inhabit this elevated plane nevertheless perceive a difference between the natural world and the supernatural. The natural has some reality for them; very little, almost imperceptible, but nevertheless some reality.

The work of this level is to attempt to break the illusion of the reality of natural cause-and-effect. The *tzaddik* who lives at this level of *emuna*, faith, is constantly working to clarify in his consciousness or to demonstrate that his natural efforts are in fact not genuine causes. He is always moving to close the gap between nature and transcendence, and the method employed in order to achieve this end is to enter the world of the natural and yet to remain aware that it is no more than the smokescreen which hides the Divine. Such a person engages the physical world whenever possible and works to remind himself (or others) of its superficiality in order to break his temptation to see it as independent. This person maximizes *hishtadlus,* natural effort, in order to break his misplaced faith in it. Before we can clarify this idea more fully, however, we must look at the next level, the third.

*   *   *

At the third level are those for whom the illusion of independence which the natural world projects is too strong, too dangerous. A person who is at this level fears that if he becomes involved in the world of natural cause-and-effect excessively he may be taken in by its appearance of solidity and independence. Such a person *minimizes* his involvement with the natural, minimizes *hishtadlus.* He is compelled to call on the miraculous instead of engaging the natural because the miraculous will certainly remind him of the true nature of the world and the Hand which wields mastery over it.

Lest we feel that this level is lowly, let us note that although the one who lives here feels unequal to the task of combating the illusion of the physical, he is nevertheless worthy of being able to cause the miraculous to manifest! Such a person desists from engaging the natural and allows the miraculous to occur in order to avoid the risk of coming to believe that his natural efforts have any intrinsic power.

*   *   *

These two levels, the second and third, are best understood by comparing them. The second is inhabited by those who do not fear that involvement with the natural is intrinsically too dangerous; for them the danger lies in slipping into unawareness of the Hand which moves the natural, and their solution is to constantly break that tendency by using the natural exactly as if it were real and independent, yet all the while reminding themselves that it is nothing.

Those who inhabit the third level, however, do not have the confidence that their use of the natural would produce such awareness. They feel that they cannot risk involvement with the physical lest its show of reality overcomes their spiritual vision. These individuals avoid the physical; they choose to allow the Divine to manifest without effort on their part in order to be forced to see the true nature of things.

Paradoxical though it may seem, the higher of these levels demands more use of the natural; the lower demands more open revelation of the miraculous.

There is a Midrash which gives classic examples of the various stages which occupy the spectrum between these two levels. Four kings of Israel are mentioned, and the Midrash brings out their respective methods of handling the problem of *hishtadlus* and *bitachon*, the problem of resolving the tension between the world of natural human effort and that of clear knowledge of the Divine behind the scenes.

King David, King Asa, King Yehoshaphat and King Chizkiyahu each requested Hashem's help in different ways – each requested a different degree of Divine intervention.

King David said: "I shall pursue my enemies and overtake them, and I shall not return until I have destroyed them." States the Midrash: "Hashem said to him 'I shall do it.'" And that is what happened; David pursued the enemy and destroyed them with Divine assistance.

King Asa said: "I do not have the power to destroy them; rather, I shall pursue them and You do it." And Hashem answered him thus: "I shall do it." Asa pursued the enemy, and Hashem destroyed them.

King Yehoshaphat said: "I do not have the power to destroy or (even) to pursue; rather, I shall sing (in prayer and praise) and You do it." And Hashem answered: "I shall do it." Yehoshaphat sang and the enemy was defeated without any military action on his part.

King Chizkiyahu said: "I do not have the power to destroy or to pursue or (even) to sing; rather, I shall sleep upon my bed, and You do it." And Hashem answered: "I shall do it." Chizkiyahu slept, and a miraculous defeat of the enemy occurred during the night.

We see four modes of conduct represented in this Midrash. King David conducts himself by fully handling the natural world – when it comes to fighting a war, he mounts a military campaign and carries out all the stages necessary. He pursues the enemy and engages them in battle. King Asa does less – he pursues the enemy, but does not do battle; when his army has pursued the enemy and overtaken them, they experience a miraculous destruction of the enemy. Yehoshaphat does even less; he does not even pursue – his actions consist of prayer and song with no attempt at military action of any kind. The result is an entirely miraculous defeat of the enemy. And King Chizkiyahu does nothing at all – when the Jewish people are threatened by an invading army, he goes to sleep! The result: during the night a miraculous rout of the enemy takes place with absolutely no human action necessary.

At first glance, it may seem that we are considering increasing levels of spiritual greatness – King David must expend much effort in order to achieve results, King Asa less, and so on. After all, King Asa is favored with a miracle, unlike King David. And King Chizkiyahu, who needs the least effort, witnesses the greatest miracle. But the truth is exactly the opposite, as our analysis of the underlying theme should have made clear: King David, at his supernal level, conducts himself within the natural realm exactly as if all consequences depend on his actions entirely, and while he is doing so *he is constantly expressing the idea that his actions are not the true cause at all.* He is using human actions to break the belief in those actions; with every flicker of every movement he declares to himself and to the world that it is only Hashem who acts in reality. Before he makes a move, states the Midrash, David calls on Hashem to do all; only then, when it is clear that whatever results is entirely Hashem's doing, does David act.

(This, in fact, is exactly what David represents – the function of the Mashiach, the Messianic King whose essence lies in the person of David himself, is to demonstrate Hashem's presence in the world.

To understand this more deeply, one may ask why the Mashiach is necessary at all – surely when the time comes for Hashem to reveal Himself openly in the world He should do so without a human representative, as it were; why is it necessary *then* to have a Messianic King? Surely that is *exactly* when human kingship should cease in order to reveal all the more clearly the true and ultimate Divine Kingship? But again, the opposite is true – the message of the Messianic King is to teach the deepest level of human striving and achievement, the ultimate purpose of human existence in its most potent form, which is the work of sacrificing the self, of yielding the ego in the service of Hashem: the Mashiach will be the most developed and exalted individual imaginable, by far the most powerful and mighty king ever to rule, *and yet he will show that he himself is empty of all independent existence;* all is Hashem, and all dominion is His. *"Ein od milvado* – There is nothing other than Him."* This is the true meaning of the Sages' statement concerning *malchus,* the concept of Kingship which is most perfectly represented by King David, as *"Leis lei mi'garmei klum* – He has nothing of his own.")

Let us return to our Midrash. As we move on through history and encounter the subsequent kings of Israel, we find that this level lessens. King Asa feels that if he makes the complete natural effort that David did, he is in danger of coming to believe, even if only minutely, that human action is an independent cause. He must limit his actions and allow the Divine to manifest miraculously in order to demonstrate clearly the true nature of reality. King Yehoshaphat feels this problem even more acutely – he knows that even a minor military action may seem to have some essential part to play in the ensuing victory; he makes no military move at all. He prays and offers song – this surely will point out unmistakably Who is in charge.

And, almost incredibly, King Chizkiyahu feels that even song would be too much – even that may be construed as effective human action intrinsically essential for the desired result; *he takes to his bed and sleeps* at the most dangerous moment preceding certain attack by a powerful enemy *in order to demonstrate absolutely unequivocally that human action is entirely superfluous in reality.*

(During King Chizkiyahu's reign the Jewish people engaged in Torah study virtually exclusively; physical effort in the realm of the natural was not the mode of conduct employed. In fact, Chizkiyahu placed a sword over the door of the *beis midrash*, the house of Torah study, and decreed that anyone who left the intense study of Torah should be pierced with it. The obvious question here is: why is desisting from Torah study punishable thus? Where do we find death by human hand as a punishment for *bitul Torah*, the neglecting of Torah study?

But the answer is clear in the light of our discussion – King Chizkiyahu's generation was entirely involved in Torah study, they did not engage in natural *hishtadlus*, natural effort in the physical. They avoided such effort; and we see from King Chizkiyahu's sword and decree that they *depended* on the very fact that they did not engage in natural effort: for them it would have been lethal to leave the *beis midrash* in order to engage in physical effort! The royal decree was in fact quite appropriate – when Torah was the full pursuit of the Jewish people, it was sufficient; but more than this: any attempt to manipulate the natural carried with it the danger of breaking the clear awareness that all is in fact dependent on the Divine hand. When it was necessary for a Jewish king to sleep in order to demonstrate the true nature of things, it would have been a treacherous and extremely dangerous act for a Jew to leave the *beis midrash* and engage in natural human effort! Such a Jew would have constituted a real threat to the safety of the nation, and a sword suspended over the *beis midrash* door indicating a royal death sentence was perfectly fitting – not for the *bitul Torah* itself, but for constituting a national danger.)

Each of these four kings makes a different type or degree of effort – King David much, King Asa less, King Yehoshaphat still less, and King Chizkiyahu none. But regardless of the degree of human effort, Hashem's response is: "I shall do it." The Midrash is teaching us that in each case, Hashem is manifesting as the true cause; the role of the human is to decide how much effort is appropriate to best demonstrate that fact.

*   *   *

There is a puzzling *gemara* which we can begin to understand using the concept we are studying. The *gemara* discusses the case of a man who lost his wife and could not afford a wet nurse to suckle his child. A miracle occurred – his breasts developed so that he himself was able to suckle the child. What is puzzling is that the *gemara* records a difference of opinion concerning this man and the miracle which was manifest for him – one opinion is "How great is that man for whom such a miracle occurred"; the second opinion is "How lowly is that man for whom the natural order of Creation was changed"!

What is the meaning of this *machlokes*, this argument? Why are the positions so radically opposed? In the light of what we have been studying, we can attempt an insight. The difference between the two positions here depends upon whether one looks at that miracle from the vantage point of our second or our third levels: from the point of view of our third level, that level at which miracles are necessary to demonstrate that nature is but a mask, such a miracle indicates greatness – after all, the man must have been very great to merit a personal miracle! "How great is that man..."

But from the point of view of our second level, that higher level at which it is appropriate to demonstrate the unreality of the natural *without recourse to miracles*, without needing miracles to break the perception of nature as real, such a miracle represents a failing. For a person who, despite his greatness, is vulnerable to the illusion of nature as an independent reality, the order of Creation must be set aside to protect him from that illusion. Relatively, such a person is lowly – he is not able to do the work of breaking the perception of nature on his own, it must be done for him. "How lowly is that man..."!

The argument here is: which is the appropriate standard with which to judge such a man and such a miracle? Is he to be looked upon from the higher standard of the second level, that level at which the power of the individual's spiritual elevation does the work of revealing the higher world unaided, or is he to be looked upon from the relatively lower level, that at which the individual must call on help from without in the form of supernatural intervention to demonstrate that same fact? At such heights of greatness, unfamiliar to the inhabitants of our generation, a miracle may represent merit and greatness, or, amazingly, it may represent a failing – the inability to achieve independently what an open and direct revelation of the Divine must achieve instead.

Before we leave these three levels of supernal greatness and study the levels that are more relevant to our generation, let us note that we have not been comparing individuals, but rather modes of conduct, modes of interacting with the world and its ordeals – the point is not whether King David was on a level higher or lower than the other great figures mentioned; the point is that either the person or the situation dictates what must be the appropriate mode of balancing *hishtadlus* and *bitachon* in order to bring out the world behind the mask.

* * *

Now we come to the fourth level, and it is here that we find most individuals. At this level, there is not the spiritual power to call miracles into existence. In fact, miracles would be entirely inappropriate here; they would serve only to lower the level of those who witnessed them. Let us study this idea.

The purpose of miracles, as we have been attempting to understand, is to benefit those who experience them. In His *hashgacha*, supervision of the world's affairs, Hashem chooses to manifest either miraculously or naturally depending on what is in the best interest of the recipients of that *hashgacha*. When Hashem reveals Himself openly, it is only for the good of those who witness that revelation. For those at the highest level of spirituality, as we have seen, miracles occur because such individuals can benefit directly from them and there is no purpose in withholding them. At the second level which we considered, miracles are not manifest because those at that level are using the natural to break its facade – miracles would deprive them of the opportunity to do that work, and these individuals achieve and generate perception of the Divine exactly because they are not living within the miraculous.

At the third level, miracles occur because those at that level gain *emuna*, faith, directly by experiencing the miraculous – every revelation of Hashem brings them into closer contact with Him; a more natural pathway would be too dangerous – it would decrease awareness of the Divine.

But for those at the fourth level, miracles do not occur *because they would be disastrous for us.* The reason is this: what would be the response of this generation if we were to witness a miraculous phenomenon? *Most of us would respond by trying to find a natural explanation for it.* And we would be held most culpable for that: if one lives within the darkness of an entirely natural-seeming world and fails to see the Divine Presence within it, one may be excused. But if one is *shown* that Presence *and then refuses to see,* that is inexcusable. When a generation is so insensitive to the spiritual that anything refined, anything higher, is made coarse and crude, then miracles are worse than wasted. Hashem is forced, as it were, to withhold Himself from revealing Himself to us because we would refuse to see! We prevent Him from manifesting; we effectively reject a relationship with Him before it can begin.

We do not merit miracles and we cannot be reached by means of miracles. We would not gain faith from miracles; but we certainly do not gain faith by their absence – those who would break even miracles down to natural proportions will certainly not elevate the natural to the miraculous! So what is left? How is Hashem to reach us, how does He make it possible for us to break through the facade of the physical? How can He sensitize people who have faith in the natural?

The answer is that He breaks the natural chain of cause-and-effect in our affairs in order to destroy our faith in it. The process is this: a person tends to believe that cause leads to effect; let us say, for example, that hard work yields success in earning a living. Every time this appears to occur, a person becomes less sensitive to the idea that Hashem is the real and immediate cause of that success, and therefore Hashem lets such a person make a proper and adequate effort which should yield handsome rewards *and then He causes that effort to fail!* The most perfectly conceived and executed business plan may fail miserably in order to teach that there is no real cause-and-effect in this area of human endeavor.

A prodigious effort may be expended to achieve a particular result and yield no fruits. When things go wrong a person should stop and ask what message is being communicated – why are such strenuous efforts ending in failure? It could be that Hashem is teaching him not to become overconfident in his own independent abilities. Failure could be the greatest gift – the gift of opened eyes.

A sensitive person will understand this and be sensitized further. When an unexpected and unnatural failure occurs, the correct attitude should be based on the realization that there is a message here: the natural is being disrupted in order to show that it is not independently reliable. This is one of the methods of helping us generate increased *emuna* when miracles cannot be employed; when it would not help to override the natural, the natural is broken.

At this level, Hashem Himself is holding up the apparent workings of the natural for human scrutiny and then breaking that natural order visibly to demonstrate its emptiness. In the very lives of those who must learn this all-important lesson it is being revealed, in their affairs and in their flesh. Here there is no work to be done to reveal the Divine or to break the natural, that is being done with no human effort; here the work is simply to see the reality that is being shown.

*   *   *

But there is a fifth level, too. What happens when a person is so stubborn that no matter what happens he refuses to see the Divine Hand? What is the pattern of Divine conduct governing the affairs of one who would not only attribute miracles to the natural but who would also insist that breaks in the usual cause-and-effect process are no more than coincidences? What can be done for an individual who just does not want to see?

The answer is that nothing can be done for him. Miracles will not help, unexpected failure will not help, and success will certainly not help – this individual would only attribute success to his own efforts and abilities. A relationship with the Divine, like any relationship, must have two sides; when one of the sides is totally unwilling, there can be no relationship.

No, nothing can be done for him; but something can be done *with* him – such people are used for a specific purpose in the world's *hashgacha*. They are used as the *temptation to lack of faith* for others: since these individuals refuse to be moved by unusual and unnatural turns of events in their affairs, Hashem *allows their affairs to run entirely predictably and naturally*. Such people may expend a great deal of effort in making a living or any other human endeavor – Hashem allows that effort to succeed exactly as if the effort is achieving the results *in order that others may have the ordeal of witnessing what seems to be the natural order of things.*

After all, the world must present a natural order if it is going to make our free will possible; these people represent the illusion of a natural order. In fact, this is no more than *midda k'neged midda,* an expression of the Divine attribute of measure for measure: such a person has chosen to become part of the natural order, to live entirely within the sphere of the physical and natural, and therefore that person is dealt with in an entirely natural way. Such a person's life will proceed naturally and predictably, subject only to the finite laws of physics and biology.

What a chilling idea: the refusal to be open to any form of communication with the spiritual results in a purely physical existence, and that very physical existence maintains and propagates the physical framework which provides the stage of free will opportunity for those who remain willing to overcome the illusion. The person who stubbornly refuses to hear any higher message has become bait on the hook of a false reality. This, at the very least, is the level to avoid.

Chapter 4

The World Parallels its Root

The Rambam states that one who asserts that the Creator has physical form forfeits his share in the next world. This applies whether the person's conception is of a physical body or any corporeal element, or even an abstract image or diagram of any sort. We are required to believe that the Creator is completely beyond any physical representation, completely transcendent, utterly incorporeal. He has no body, no tangible aspect, and no parts.

The problem, however, is that *the Torah speaks of Hashem as if He were physical* – many verses speak of Hashem's hand, His arm, His eyes and many other such attributes. "With a mighty hand and an outstretched arm;" "The eyes of Hashem... are upon it (the Land of Israel)." If we are forbidden to conceive of any corporeal or particulate image when relating to Hashem, why does the Torah do so? We know that Hashem obeys His own rules, as it were, He observes the Torah's commandments; why not this one?

Why, and indeed how, are we expected to relate to the Divine utilizing no picture or image at all *when the Torah itself does*?

The sin of *hagshama* – attributing physical properties to Hashem – is very serious indeed; one who prays to Hashem while picturing some image or form is transgressing this prohibition, and it is in the category of idolatry. Why then does the Torah, Hashem's own teaching, speak in graphic and corporeal images? What exactly is one supposed to picture when reading verses which openly mention Hashem's hand or foot? And again, if it is forbidden to conceptualize a hand or a foot, why does the Torah express itself thus?

The Rambam himself deals with this question. In *Hilchos Y'sodei ha'Torah* (the Laws of the Fundamentals of Torah) he states: "*Dibra Torah k'lashon b'nei adam* – the Torah speaks in human terms." This would appear to mean that the Torah is speaking metaphorically when it mentions Divine attributes in human terms; the Torah is "borrowing" human language.

At first glance it seems that the Torah speaks this way because we cannot understand any other method of expression; we can understand only those things which are part of our world. We live in a finite, differentiated world; we are familiar with beings who have hands, eyes and feet – and therefore the Torah speaks to us in terms which are familiar to us. After all, how could the Torah speak any other way and be comprehensible by finite beings? Of course, we understand that beyond the metaphor, beyond the borrowed language, there is much more – the finite words of Torah clothe endless layers of deeper meaning; the outer layer is only the vehicle, so to speak, for the deeper meaning.

But since abstraction cannot be expressed except through concrete means, the Torah speaks in those concrete terms which are familiar to us.

However, deeper thought will show that this cannot be correct. If the Rambam means that the Torah is using human terms as analogy, as *mashal*, we are faced with two major difficulties. Firstly, how can the Torah speak in terms which are not strictly true? We know that the Torah is true in the very deepest sense possible; every nuance within Torah must be true. Since the Torah is none other than Hashem Himself speaking, *even the outermost layers of its expression must be absolutely accurate and true.* Analogies and metaphors may be useful, but they are not true in themselves. If the Torah wants us to understand something very deep and abstract when it talks of Hashem's hand, for example, that is fine, but how can it speak of a hand *if the simple meaning of that word is not literally true as well?* Put another way: if Hashem does not really have a hand, but the Torah says that He does because we are limited to finite and familiar concepts, is this not in some sense inaccurate, false? Is untruth justified because we cannot hear truth? Surely not!

And secondly, apart from the problem of the falsehood of attributing physical properties to the Divine, it is forbidden! We are not allowed to conceive of Hashem as possessing any human or physical properties; why does the Torah apparently do just that? We are expected to relate to Hashem without imagining any finite form; why does the Torah describe such form? Again, surely the deficiency of our understanding would not justify the Torah's doing something which itself is a Torah prohibition?

*   *   *

There is a solution to this problem which is found in those sources which deal with such problems; but although it is true, the deeper sources indicate that it is not enough to answer our question fully. This approach understands that when the Torah mentions attributes of Hashem such as His hand or His eye, it is referring to what are known as *hanhagos* – Hashem's conduct of the world and His actions within it. Understood thus, Hashem's hand would mean His actions within the physical realm, His eyes would mean that He sees what occurs in the world, and so on.

Now while this way of understanding our subject may be true, those sources which reach into the deepest realms of Torah thought indicate that it does not adequately solve our problem, and the reason is this: If Hashem's hand is understood to mean a *hanhaga*, a mode of conduct within the world, that is true only within the world. *However, the Torah indicates that Hashem Himself* has a hand; not only where His actions can be apprehended by human awareness, but even far above the zone of our perception and existence, in Hashem's intrinsic Being, as it were, in that ineffable and holy Being which is indicated by Hashem's Name of essence itself.

In other words, if the Torah talks of Hashem's hand, it *must* mean that He has a hand, intrinsically and most literally. It is not enough to say that the Torah is referring to something within the world when it mentions Divine attributes; the Torah's expression is clear: if it states that even above the finite world there are specific features, it must be so.

*   *   *

We shall need to seek more deeply. There is a more accurate answer to our question, and one who hears it will find his perception of reality forever changed.

How can Hashem have a real hand? Surely a real hand is finite, physical, a contradiction to the infinite Oneness of the Creator? Surely the Divine hand must be some sort of *mashal*, analogy? But the secret which answers our question is this: *Hashem's hand is a real hand and our human hand is a mashal!* When the Torah talks of the Divine hand it is referring to that which is real in the deepest sense; that which is *infinite and no contradiction* to the absolute Oneness of the Creator. Every nuance of meaning in Torah is absolutely true; Hashem indeed has a hand – but that hand transcends human understanding no less than any other Divine attribute which is expressed in Torah, and no less than what we refer to as Hashem Himself.

Of course, this means that we cannot begin to understand any of the Divine attributes mentioned in the Torah. Since they are all real and essential, and since they all live in that realm of Oneness which has no parts, they do not contradict the idea of the Oneness of the Creator. And no human mind can begin to imagine the meaning of that which is described as specific or particular and yet does not contradict the fundamental element of Torah faith which is exactly the idea of that Oneness.

So we can say that Hashem has a hand, but we cannot understand what that means. And that is exactly the point: *the reason that we have been created with hands is so that we can begin to understand!* We possess parts, components, differentiated aspects of our bodies so that we can begin to fathom the meaning of these things at their root. *We are the mashal!* Hashem wants us to begin to understand Him; part of the purpose of learning Torah is to begin to understand what a human can understand of the Divine; and therefore we are given the tangible tools that we need.

*　　*　　*

In fact, this idea extends far beyond the human body: all of the world is an analogy for a higher reality. Each detail of the world teaches something about its source in the spiritual world; each detail here is an exact parallel of that which exists there. This is perfectly logical: if we were commanded to study and understand the spiritual realm and yet had no avenue of access to that understanding, what would be the sense of such a command? The pathway to deeper insight is clear: we are in fact enjoined to see more deeply, to look into those depths that cannot be seen by human eyes, and the access is by means of a close and sensitive study of that which is revealed.

Just as a person observes the physical body of his friend in order to relate to the *person* or the inner being of that friend, so too we study the structure and movements of the physical world in order to perceive its root. The truth is that there is no other way; a person never sees the inner being or *neshama* of another person – we simply have no sense-organ which can directly perceive a soul. All we can do is observe the person's bodily expression sensitively and we automatically gain insight into who they *are*. Subtle movements of the body, a subtle flicker of expression on the face, an almost imperceptible smile or motion of acceptance, the slightest gesture of tension or relaxation in bodily posture – all of these speak worlds.

All communication between people occurs thus. Speech itself is none other than the physical moving of tongue and lips generating sound waves which cause a physical response in the ear of the listener. The wonder is that subtle and refined ideas can be translated from their native medium in the mind and reduced to these physical forms. But there is no other way – the only access we have to the thoughts and personality of another human being is through the vehicle of the concrete, the physical.

In relating to people, that switch from outer body to inner person is achieved effortlessly: when relating intensely to another person one is usually unaware of the interface provided by the body, one simply perceives the inner reality *as if* directly. This natural ability to use the medium of the body to see its core is itself a Divine gift which teaches us that such perception can be achieved. *The challenge is to use the entire world in this way;* all aspects of the physical world should be engaged and studied for what they reveal about their Creator.

This is a remarkable and inspiring view of the world: every object and phenomenon it contains is a Divine lesson, a *mashal* relating to the Creator. He so to speak clothes Himself in a body which is the Universe and asks us to study that body carefully. And from each flicker of movement in that cosmic body we learn about that which pertains to Him. He in His essence is unfathomable to us; while we inhabit physical forms we cannot perceive the transcendent directly just as we cannot perceive the soul of a human directly. But just as we can perceive the human soul by means of its vehicle, the body, so too can we begin to perceive the Divine root of the world by means of that vehicle, that body which we call the world.

                              *   *   *

A *mashal* for this *mashal* is appropriate. Consider
images projected on a screen: the forms and figures moving
on the screen are no more than light dancing in two
dimensions. They may look very convincing, and one may
even forget for a while that they are only pictures. But in fact
those images are very distant versions of the people and
places photographed to produce them. However, and this is
the critical point to remember, *they are exact replicas of the
original.*

They may be entirely illusory compared to their
sources, but one who carefully studies that light dancing on
that screen *will recognize those people and places when he meets
them in the future.*

The analogy is clear: one who studies this world well is
studying that which is a distant representation of a source
which cannot be seen from here. But one day in the future,
on that inevitable day when the transition must be made
from this world to another, the one who has studied well
will recognize every detail of reality. Then it will become
apparent that this world, for all its beauty and sense of
reality, is in depth a *mashal* for the Divine Source of that
reality.
                              *   *   *

Every human experience holds and teaches more than
it seems to contain at first glance. Every human experience is
none other than the finite translation of an infinite idea.
Human consciousness, while locked into a physical body,
interprets deeper experience as superficial experience; our

work is to translate that superficial experience back into its source in depth.

One can acquire a unique insight into the world in a manner which powerfully builds *emuna*, faith, by examining all of human experience in the light of this idea. Why do we laugh? Why do we cry? Why do we long to travel and yet long for home when we are away? Each of these phenomena, and in fact every detail of human behavior and response, reveals a source in the *neshama* which yields an immeasurable bounty of spiritual understanding. We cannot here examine each of the facets of experience, but perhaps one or two will suffice as illustrations.

Why do we long for home? It is a universal human experience that when one is away from one's home, and particularly from the home of one's youth, one longs to be back there. A place has special beauty in the eyes of those who live there, even when that place has no particular natural beauty. *"Chen makom al yosh'vav –* A place has special beauty for those who live in it." If all of our experiences are none other than this-worldly parallels of higher experiences, what does this mean? The answer is that the *neshama* is derived from a higher world; its true place, its true home, is that world where it enjoyed indescribable closeness with its Creator. It is sent into this world, immeasurably distant from that place of origin, to reside in the body of a mortal being. But it never forgets its home; it forever longs with a most powerful longing to return. However, this depth remains subconscious; the *neshama* longs for its real home in the spiritual realm but the emotions read that longing as homesickness! After all, the realm of origin is not visible from here; the *neshama* has lost sight of it, the mind cannot see it. And so the conscious mind interprets that deep experience of origin as a particular facet of the human psyche familiar to each of us.

And when we are home we long to travel! For all the *neshama's* love of its origin, it nevertheless longs to move through this world, distant from its home, to enjoy the beauty of this world and to acquire its wealth – the true wealth of *mitzvos* and perfection of character. (In fact, the very trait of acquisitiveness is none other than the *neshama's* interpretation of this depth!) The explicit, conscious psyche experiences this deep stirring of the *neshama* as wanderlust, the longing to travel.

Each facet of human behavior and emotion must be studied closely for the clues it holds. No detail of the psyche or of the world is accidental, coincidental. If the world is a projection of a deeper reality, then each detail reveals the reality that projects it.

And all of this is to give us the clues we need to uncover origins; our own, and those of the world in its entirety.

*　　*　　*

So we understand that all of our experiences are projections of reality which teach us abou that reality. If this is true, then we must face a perplexing question: if every human experience is an illusion relative to its source in the higher world, *what is a dream?* What does a dream teach us about reality? If our experiences here are relatively illusory, why would Hashem have created us with dreams as part of our lives – a dream is all illusion; why put illusion into the illusion? Let us understand: in a dream, one is not aware that one is dreaming – the dream seems very real, sometimes ecstatically pleasurable, sometimes terrifyingly traumatic.

The very intensity of these feelings is due to the fact that one perceives them as fully alive and real. And yet when one wakes, perhaps sitting up in bed in a sweat generated by the torment of a nightmare, one is relieved to realize that what one has just gone through was only a dream. Why do we need this experience of the unreal which seems so real?

The answer is clear and illuminating. Imagine for a moment an uninformed person being told about the nature of life in this world and the transition from this world to the next. Imagine that such a person is being told: "You should know that this world is only an illusion relative to the next. It may seem real, but do not be fooled – one day, sooner or later, you will leave this dimension and enter an entirely different one. There you will realize that all you have experienced in life was a very faint echo of the reality you perceive there. That is real life; whatever you knew before was almost nothing in comparison to it."

The person being told this story would probably reply: "That sounds wild! How can I accept such an idea? Surely it is more reasonable for me to see the world in terms of what meets the eye right now; how can I believe that all my awareness of the world is only an illusion? That is simply outside of my experience and outside of all the evidence available to me. I reject such fanciful and unsubstantiated stories!"

And one would certainly be excused for replying thus! A person could not possibly be expected to doubt his perception of the world with which he has such solid contact. Since all his senses assure him that his experience of the world is true and reliable, he could not think otherwise.

Unless he has ever had a dream! Anyone who has ever dreamed has *experienced* the remarkable transition from what seems completely real to a state in which it is obvious that the reality of which he was so sure a few seconds before was entirely an illusion! After living through a few vivid dreams a person *must* be faced with a very unsettling thought: when you dream, for argument's sake let us say a terrifying dream, and you awake and sit upright in bed still sweating and shaking, you are enormously relieved to realize that it was only a dream and that now you are awake. But *are you sure*? Can you be sure? How do you know that you are awake now – because you simply know, you can feel clearly that you are awake? But in your dream you were certain that you were awake too!

Anyone who has dreamed has experienced the priceless gift of feeling in the flesh, in the most immediate way, that the state of being which we call life in this world has no inherent assurance of being objectively real and permanent. The briefest dream kills forever the smug self-assurance of the attitude that would otherwise be natural – that my experience is perfectly reliable and that I experience the only reality that there is. A dream is a humbling experience. And it is the key to belief in a world after this one; it is an experience in this world that should sensitize us to the idea that there is more to life here than meets the eye. No one who has dreamed can possibly deny that with any confidence at all.

And so even a dream, that experience of illusion, teaches about reality! Dreams do not break the rule: every human experience is an opportunity to learn *emuna*.

Chapter 5

Levels of Order

The world is exquisitely ordered; the very fact that it can be studied mathematically and scientifically results from this order. If the world parallels its spiritual root, and we wish to understand that root, we must study the order inherent in the world.

The world (and the human mind) contains three levels of order:

I.

The first, *seder l'shem seder*, order for the sake of order, is the symmetry and harmony apparent in the world. This natural order permeates the entire universe; in fact, this level of order *is the structure of the universe*. The outer world always parallels the inner: if the outer world is structured, the mind must be so too, and it is this very order of the mind, reflecting the order of the physical world, which makes it possible to think logically and consistently. We have ordered pathways in our minds, and we perceive the ordered organization of the world.

There is a fascinating resonance to these inner and outer patterns of order: when they are in harmony with each other, we perceive their harmonious dance; when they are in disharmony, we perceive their dissonance. If one is in a situation where order or symmetry is apparent, one's response to that symmetry will depend on one's own inner sense of order or lack of it. For example, if one is travelling by train and is aware of the symmetrical rhythm of the wheels on the tracks – *clickety-click, clickety-click, clickety-click* – one's response to that rhythm depends on one's own inner rhythm at the time: if one is at peace, inwardly tranquil, as one may be when travelling towards some pleasantly anticipated destination, the sound is soothing, pleasant, even musical. The inner symmetry and the outer symmetry are resonating in harmony. But if one is in distress inwardly, perhaps travelling to some unpleasant or feared destination, and one's thoughts and emotions are in turmoil, *the sound is unbearable.* The outer harmony is mocking the inner disharmony, and we feel the pain of that mockery.

If a person enters his home in a fine, serene mood after a productive and uncomplicated day, and notices one item of furniture slightly out of place – one of the chairs around the table not quite in line with the others – he may walk over and adjust it so that everything is perfect. His inner order seeks to be mirrored in the outer world. But if the same person enters his home at the end of a frustrating, disastrous day and finds everything just as it should be – all the chairs perfectly in line – he may storm over and kick them into total disarray. The perfect symmetry of his environment mocks the disorder within his mind and the result is an angry attempt to reduce all order into chaos. Of course, it is not only furniture which may be angrily treated at such times – all too often it is people: usually those who are closest and deserve it least. The disharmonious relationship with self spills over into disharmonious relationships with others.

A fractured inner world reflects itself in outer breakdown; a healthy inner world reflects itself in outer order. It is said that when Rabbi Simcha Zissel, a master of *mussar* (Jewish character-building), would visit his son in yeshiva, he would enter the boy's dormitory room and note the state of the room. If his son's shoes were neatly together under the bed, he would leave without seeing him. He knew that if his son's possessions were neat and organized, so was his mind; there was no need to disturb his studies!

*   *   *

This understanding of the relationship between inner and outer structures yields an insight into modern Western society. A society has an inner ethos or consciousness and an outer expression. If we wish to explore the consciousness of a generation, we must study its expression in its art forms and its behavior. If art is an expression of the mind and the heart of the artist, then the art of a society will be a reflection of that society's collective mind and heart.

If we trace the development of all the art forms in Western culture over the past four or five centuries, we find a remarkable thing. In every art form, there has been a striking movement from order to disorder. This is not the place for a detailed analysis of the history of art, but a brief overview will illustrate our point.

In music, for example, the Baroque period was characterized by a highly structured style, meticulous in its rhythmicity and mathematical pattern. In the subsequent Classical period there was a freer style; however, structure was still paramount. The Romantic period allowed more freedom, but rules of form and style were observed. As we move into the modern period, we find an accelerating abandoning of structure – Impressionist composers moved away from the constraints of convention and produced music which was atonal; one of the best-known Impressionist composers had to be escorted from the concert hall by police after the first performance of his major composition – the audience was so outraged that they attacked him! The outrage generated by producing music which departed from familiar keys and rules of rhythm soon gave way to acceptance, however, and in the modern era it is perfectly acceptable to write and perform music which has no system of convention at all. A modern composer writes music on a mobile: as the staves move in the breeze in front of the musician he plays whatever he sees crossing his field of vision. Another places a cat on the piano keyboard and proceeds to prick it with a pin: as the cat attempts to escape, the audience listens to the sounds produced and ponders their meaning.

The same progression can be seen in painting. Commenting on the nature of modern art, one wry critic observed that there was once a time when a painting of a bowl of fruit looked like a bowl of fruit! In fact, painting a few centuries ago was all representational; the artist's skill was devoted to capturing a living likeness. Any objective viewer would certainly recognize the result. As we follow painting into the more modern era, however, we find that the concern of the artist became to capture some or other aspect of his subject, not necessarily in harmony with its totality but rather as a subjective experience; and in the most modern phase, the artist will often choose to portray total disharmony.

A visit to a gallery of modern art will reveal canvases with splatters of paint, perhaps various materials glued to a canvas apparently haphazardly, or a wall-sized canvas with a single spot of color in one corner. A modern artist may paint blindfolded or walk around on the canvas with paint on his feet to achieve an effect. The results are often bizarre; there can be little question that if such works would have been displayed two or three centuries ago they would have been deemed to be the work of deranged minds.

If art is a reflection of the collective mind of a culture or a generation, then the conclusion is unavoidable: a taste for symmetry and structure surely implies an inner sense of these qualities, and a taste, or at least an acceptance, of disharmony and destructuring implies a breakdown of the inner sense of order. Whether expressions of discord and disharmony such as those of the modern era are rightfully to be termed art or not is not the point of this discussion; the point is simply that the creative expression of this generation reflects a preoccupation with such dissonances.

The same pattern can be discerned in the development of all the arts. In poetry, for example, four hundred years ago all English poetry was written in strict accord with the rules of rhythm and meter. The various forms of poetry were defined by their pattern – a sonnet is a very particular form of poem, and all sonnets were written in the classical form of a sonnet. All poetry observed rules. In modern poetry, however, there are no set rules at all. Much of modern poetry is written in flagrant breach of the most basic rules of English, let alone poetry. A modern poem may have lines of varying length, no capital letters, no rhyme scheme and no fixed rhythm. Again, the point is not whether this is good poetry or not; the point is simply that order and symmetry have given way to disorder.

A study of drama yields the same observation. Early drama was highly organized, even stylized. A comedy had certain defining characteristics, so did a tragedy. A student of drama could identify the characteristic elements of a particular work of drama with ease. The dramatist's skill lay in using a set form creatively, not in developing new forms. Modern drama, however, often follows no rules. "Theater of the Absurd" is a perfect illustration – in this modern form, a play may have no plot at all. In fact, part of the idea behind such works is the very lack of structure. Such a play may consist of two characters speaking their lines from within two garbage cans for the duration of the play, or consist of characters waiting hopelessly for a redemption that never comes. The message is clear: existential anxiety drives the creative effort and the medium reflects the message.

Architecture and interior design are not exceptions. A visitor to Wordsworth's house in England's Lake District notes an interesting feature on being shown into the ornate drawing room. As one enters the room through a door at one end, one finds that in the wall directly opposite there is an identical door. But that door is a fake – it leads nowhere. The reason: in the era during which that house was built and appointed it was unthinkable to decorate a room asymmetrically! If there is a door in this wall, there must be a matching, balancing one exactly opposite. Anyone inhabiting such a dwelling then would have felt uncomfortable in asymmetrical surroundings.

Yet today, design is almost never symmetrical. The modern eye finds absolute symmetry boring in the extreme. It is common today to find walls of different colors in the same room, unusual angles and unbalanced shapes used for interest. The modern psyche is comfortable in a disordered environment.

The same point can be made for sculpture. Classically, sculpture was entirely representational. The great works of previous generations were great exactly for their accurate representation of natural forms. Modern sculpture does not attempt this – a modern exhibition of sculpture is likely to feature piles of twisted metal welded into abstract shapes, parts of dismantled machinery arranged haphazardly, or consist of mobile parts moving in no particular pattern.

One could devote far more time to an analysis of this phenomenon; the point, however, should be clear.

If it is true that the inner state seeks to be reflected in the outer form, then we can begin to understand – as the Messianic age approaches, as mankind devolves into pre-Messianic strife and disintegration, the artistic expression of society accurately reveals the inner turmoil. Technological advances have not been paralleled by moral and spiritual advance, and the existential vacuum breeds a directionless disarray.

II.

The second, *seder l'shem totz'osav*, order for the sake of its results, is that type of order in which parts are arranged in such a way that they function. The purpose of the organization of the components is to maintain the proper relationship between them so that each can fulfill its function correctly. An example of this kind of order is a library which is indexed. The index contains the order of the library; it makes each book accessible. The index is the key to the successful functioning of the library: without it, all the books may be useless. The system requires that all the books be arranged correctly and that the index reflects their arrangement.

Rabbi Elchanan Wasserman used to point out that if a library has an index, the more books it contains, the better; however, when the index is lacking, the more books the library comprises, the worse! Without an index to enable the user to find the particular book which he needs, the sheer number of the books becomes the problem. And thus it is, he would explain, with the order inherent in the human mind: the more organized the mind, the more useful are many facts. But the undisciplined, disorganized mind is better off with fewer facts – they are more likely to be accessible in their disarray when they are few in number. One who wishes to know much must first develop structured and orderly thinking.

III.

The third type of order, *seder l'shem achdus ha'peula*, order for the sake of unity of function, is a higher level of order. Here, the components of a whole are organized and connected in such a way that they blend into a unified entity. This composite entity functions precisely because of the harmonious blending of its components.

An example of this type of order would be a complex machine – the parts of the machine are interconnected in such a way that the machine functions properly. Each part would be useless on its own, but together they achieve their purpose. This is not to be confused with the order of the previous level: the type of order which an index imposes on a library ensures the function of the library as a whole, but each book in the library has its own separate identity and use – even if the index disappears and the books become completely disorganized, each book remains a book; however, in the case of a machine, the individual parts are *nothing* on their own; it is only in their interconnectedness that they achieve any meaning at all. In the library, the index makes each self-contained part accessible and therefore useful; but in the machine, the order and organization are the *entire reason* for the existence of the parts; no individual part has any use without all the others.

In an engine, for example, there may be a small screw in the carburettor which is almost insignificant in terms of its intrinsic value – it may be worth less than the smallest coin. But without it the engine does not run; and if that small screw were to fall out when the vehicle powered by that engine were in an inhospitable and dangerous place, the hapless driver may feel that it is worth the value of the entire vehicle. Without that tiny part he has nothing at all. While the engine was running smoothly that part was unconsidered and unappreciated; now that it is missing its value has become apparent.

Systems which are set up in such a way that all the parts are needed before any become relevant have a unique quality: each part manifests a paradoxical duality. Each part is at one and the same time nothing and everything: nothing because it is only a part, without the rest of the system it is utterly useless; and everything because when all the other parts are in place and functioning, it becomes essential and critical. Each part depends on all the others entirely, in this it is utterly subservient; and yet all the others depend on it, in this it is utterly controlling.

* * *

Such a system is the Jewish people. Each individual Jew is essential and unique, utterly necessary for the cosmic purpose which the Jewish nation must manifest, and yet lost in his merely biological smallness when not fulfilling his destiny as a Jew. In fact, at a broader scale, all of mankind and the Universe constitute such a system: everything in the world is created unique in its position and function and will ultimately reveal how critically necessary it is in the greater scheme of reality.

When the Jewish people travelled through the desert they travelled in formation – the *diglei midbar*, or "flags of the desert"; each tribe occupied a specific position within the camp. The root of this formation lies in the fact that each tribe has a specific identity and function within the Jewish people and therefore a specific place. Within each tribe, each family has a specific and unique role, and so too each individual within each family. As the Jewish people were being formed the uniqueness of each element within the nation was being laid down.

* * *

As individuals who form a whole in such a way that each of us is critically important, we reflect this principle in our emotions. As we have seen previously, the human psyche is a reflection of the deeper energies of Creation which it comprises, and study of its details yields deep knowledge of the world.

It is a feature of our emotional makeup that we respond both to the experience of being unique and single, and also to the experience of blending into a team or crew. Actually, these responses are antithetical: if it is natural to thrill to the experience of being a single, all-important individual, there should be a negative response to losing one's identity in a group; yet we find, paradoxically, that both are thrilling.

For example, in a situation where disaster is imminent, all present are immobilized by fear or surprise, and one acts decisively and heroically and saves the day unaided, such an event yields a great thrill; in fact, such is the stuff of many a young person's fantasy. There is a special thrill in the awareness that the entire deliverance depended on one individual; the very aloneness of that individual in acting is the source of that unique surge of ego-experience.

However, it is also a clear feature of human consciousness that we thrill to experiences in which the individual parts blend into a harmonious whole in such a way that the parts become locked into the whole indistinguishably: a mass display of precision gymnastics in which no individual stands out but the entire human mass seems to function as one being, for example, evokes a special feeling in both the participants and the onlookers. Certain team sports which depend on perfect interaction between members of the team provide a unique thrill. In such activities, if one member were to make a small move expressing his particular individual existence, the entire experience would be destroyed.

Precision aerobatics and other displays of precise teamwork evoke this response. Men marching in perfect step in a battalion of thousands describe a remarkable feeling of becoming larger than a single individual; the experience can be powerful.

We respond in these two seemingly opposite ways because that is exactly the nature and purpose of the human experience: each of us is unique, cosmically important; yet we achieve our uniqueness precisely when we fit into a larger order perfectly. Remarkably, it is exactly when we blend into the Universal picture exactly as we should in terms of our private, unique qualities and abilities that we thrill to the realization that no-one else could fulfill this particular function, no-one else could stand exactly here and do what must be done here. I fit in perfectly so that I become indistinguishable as an individual, and yet in so doing my individuality swells to the proportions of the Universe. I am nothing, and yet I am everything. Each person reflects the uniqueness of the image of the Creator; the totality of the Universe reflects the Oneness of the Creator; and in depth, the two are not in contradiction.

*   *   *

This idea gives rise to insights into the work of each individual. First, one must strive to discover one's uniqueness. What is my particular task? What essential part of the Universe is mine to build? This question is critically important – a life spent pursuing some unrealistic and inappropriate goal is a life wasted, and worse, damages the entire structure. When that small and seemingly insignificant screw in the carburettor of that engine which we considered previously falls out of place and rattles around in the cylinders, for example, the entire engine may be irreparably damaged.

Second, one must realize that the thrill of fitting in is a much more mature experience than the thrill of being a loner at any cost: the immature personality will choose to step *out of line* in order to experience its own uniqueness; the fact that the overall structure is being betrayed and damaged is not relevant to such an undeveloped mind. Immaturity cannot see the beauty in yielding the self in order to actualize the self; in truth, however, that is the only way to genuine selfhood.

A fascinating feature of Torah life is that it is normative in its practice and yet it develops sharply individualistic personalities. This would seem to be paradoxical, but it is fact. Torah living demands attention to fine detail in everyday living, and in fact the secular prediction might be that people who conduct themselves according to closely defined *halachic* norms would turn out to be robotic clones of the same pattern. Such a prediction would seem to make sense. And yet the opposite is true: highly developed Torah personalities are strikingly individualistic, as anyone who moves in the Torah world knows.

Study and expression of that reflection of the Universe which is Torah leads to a sure grasp of individual purpose and identity. Torah life hones and shines individual greatness, and yet orchestrates the individual elements into a great harmony.

Chapter 6

Hidden World, Revealed World

I.

Let us look more closely at the duality of hidden, inner world and revealed, outer world. *"Ein ha'bracha m'tzuya ela b'davar ha'samui min ha'ayin –* Blessing is not found except in that which is hidden from the eye." When a thing is revealed in the outer, finite world it becomes limited to the proportions of the finite environment in which it finds itself. But while a thing is hidden, while it yet lives in the unlimited, unrevealed world it has none of the constraints of the finite.

In the world of potential all things can exist, but in the physical world only one version of a thing can exist at any one time. For any thing to manifest in the material world, all that it could have been must be sacrificed except that solitary version of itself which manifests here. Here things are crystallized, frozen into physical form, and the physical can be only one thing at a time.

The body lives in the outer world. It is physical, it can be perceived easily, mechanically, with finite tools. The *neshama* (soul), the personality, lives in the inner dimension; it can be perceived *only* with an inner faculty. There are no tools which can be used to perceive the *neshama* directly. The tools needed are inner sensitivity, refined spirituality, a sense of the unlimited. The tools must fit the task.

The world consists of this duality – the inner *neshama* dimension and the body. The inner dimension moves, motivates, *is* the meaning; the body expresses the *neshama*, brings it into the world, *reveals* the meaning. At the macroscopic level, this duality describes the Universe – the Divine Presence is the hidden, inner energy; the physical world is His expression. The inner world is male; it holds the seed of potential. The outer world is female; it gives shape and expression to that potential. (In fact, we refer to Hashem as male and the world as female.)

*   *   *

We live in a generation which emphasizes the external. Torah values are diametrically opposed to those of modern secular culture; Torah eyes focus on the inner world. Even when dealing with external things, the goal should be to use those things as avenues to the inner reality.

In modern society, all that has to do with women is immodestly exposed. In Torah society there is an extreme sensitivity to this; since woman is the one who brings into the finite (the word *n'keva*, female, literally means to fix, to make finite – as in the verse *"nak'va scharcha alai v'etena* – Fix your wage and I shall pay it"), she is the one who knows how to guard the hidden dimension, to guard her privacy.

The exposing of women is a sure sign of a society which focuses on externality; the maintaining of woman's modesty is a feature of a society which values spirituality above the physical.

*   *   *

In the non-Torah world the physical aspect of the human is intensively studied and probed, but the inner aspect is either neglected or seen as secondary. The current ethos asserts that we are no more than accidental biological entities; if there is any inner dimension it is considered to be no more than a collection of instincts directing the organism's behavior.

The truth is that investigation of the inner world of the mind and *neshama* requires sensitive tools. The tools appropriate to observation and investigation of the outer world are generally useless for looking inward, and when the wrong tools are used, the results are certain to be paradoxical and senseless. Since the view current in this era is that the only reliable tools are those of the scientific laboratory, these are the tools applied to the human mind and its behavior, and the results are predictable. The nature of free will and spiritual striving are such that they are not amenable to the kind of scientific enquiry which is valid when investigating the body, and when they are assessed as if they inhabit the same realm as the physical body, they are shrunk to finite proportions and misunderstood. Again, the tools must be appropriate for the task.

When man is studied by means of the same technical tools as are used to study animals, for example, the conclusion must be that man is purely biological. Electrodes inserted into the human brain will never show more than biological activity identical to that of an animal. The point which makes us different from the animal is that point which lies above the biological plane, that area of the mind which precedes mechanical thought and brain activity, and that rarefied zone is not measurable with electrodes or any other physical tool. It must be accessed with non-physical tools, and those tools are developed by Torah study and practice. There is simply no other avenue into the inner world; it can be grasped only in its own terms.

II.

Current values hold that we are animals. All of our activities including all of our inner lives are seen as purely mechanical, serving no more than the function of survival. Our responses and emotions cannot be understood to have any absolute meaning; they are only the result of a long series of accidental developments. Man is therefore accidental, purposeless, and essentially animal.

However, even those who most strenuously assert the animal nature of man usually live as if life has some higher meaning and value. Some of the most scientifically-minded and non-spiritual investigators are champions of civil rights, for example. Of course, if man is purely animal, there can be no such thing as civil rights; if monkeys cannot meaningfully be said to have any rights in the deeper sense, then such a concept cannot exist in the human realm either – when did rights evolve in the random and mechanical process which purportedly gave rise to the human organism? Surely human rights, or any other value which humans hold dear, can never be more than simply mechanics of group interaction similar to the mechanics which govern ant colonies or cattle herds. Values based on truth or justice or any higher concept can have absolutely no place in the human system – if they are non-existent in the animal realm they cannot suddenly become real in any higher sense in the human realm.

When a scientist asserts that he is seeking the truth in an idealistic sense, he is asserting that he is not animal – no animal searches for anything in the world of values. It is inconsistent for a purely scientific investigator who denies any transcendent possibility to search for anything higher than the mechanical, or in fact to subscribe to anything at all in the world of values or meaning. But the fact is that deep in the heart of man lies a certain conviction *that there is meaning*, that he is not animal. And it is this disquieting knowledge which leads all but the most existentially committed and convinced (and convincing) secular mind into the realm of the search for truth and the assertion of essentially human values even though that realm is inconsistent with the accidental and the animal.

Many comm tted evolutionists live as if their lives and relationships have meaning. Intellectually, they may reason (and teach) that all their sense of meaning comprises is purely mechanical survival instinct, but they cannot live that way. Even the most hardened advocate of a purely biological base for man's existence suffers uniquely spiritual pain when his relationships enter difficulties. Such a biologist may teach that human love is no more than an evolutionary mating instinct sophisticated by long eons of mammalian development, but when his wife enters an adulterous relationship with one of his associates, he does not respond with the equanimity of a gorilla in the jungle watching the biological cavortings of other gorillas. Of course, when he catches himself feeling thus humanly vulnerable he will reason intellectually that the whole matter is only biological, but he will never be convinced in the depth of his inalienably human soul.

In fact, the very agonizing over these existential questions is uniquely human, and yet powerful intellects continue to assert that there is no more to such thoughts than random biological processes. Sometimes the paradox is striking: a certain Rabbi was recently travelling by air when the woman next to him was served a vegetarian airline meal. He enquired of her whether she was eating such food for religious reasons – perhaps she was Jewish and concerned about kosher food? "No," she replied, expressing her purely vegetarian motive and her indignation at those who eat animal products: "I do not eat other animals." The Rabbi answered her in a kindly way; but the correct answer to that statement is: "Why not? Other animals do!"

That vegetarian is living an intense paradox. Seeing herself as part of the family of animals and therefore feeling the injustice of eating animal food *is a uniquely human thing* – no animal has such compunctions! It is precisely *because she is not an animal* that she holds such a moral position. The merits of vegetarianism are not at issue here; the point is what exactly constitutes the essence of being human, and the very agonizing over such issues is the hallmark of a creature who is anything but animal.

Chapter 7

Words - Real and Unreal

I.

In Torah, words always express essence, and close study of the words is rewarded by an understanding of the nature of the ideas which those words describe. In the secular world, words are also revealing: the language of a culture reveals its heart. If one inclines a sensitive ear to the expression of ideas within a society one gains insight into its values.

In Torah, words express essence because words are in fact the basis for the existence of those things which they describe: the world was created by Hashem's *saying* the words which themselves became the objects of Creation. In Hebrew, the word for a "word" and for a "thing" are the same – *"davar"*; all things in the world are in fact none other than Divine words crystallized into material existence. The words are the medium of Creation, and a correct grasp of the words is a correct grasp of the elements of Creation.

Now there is a fascinating class of words which exist in the language of the secular culture in which we live which have no equivalent in Torah. There is no translation of these terms into authentic Hebrew – no source is to be found in Scripture. Many of these words represent central ideas within society, and yet they exist only outside of Torah.

What is the meaning of a word which does not exist in Torah, in the language of Creation? The inescapable answer is that, somehow, such words are describing things which are not part of the original Creation, not part of the real world. They do not represent Divine energy which has crystallized into existence; they cannot represent more than the human source which invents them. They may convey concepts which are clear within the context of a culture, but the fact that the language of Creation and essence does not contain them reveals that *they convey illusory ideas*. They may exist in the imagination of people, they may describe and motivate human behavior and action, but they are essentially of human manufacture.

In fact, within Torah thought we find words which have no Scriptural source but which were coined by the Sages – such words describe concepts which are clear to the human mind but have no absolute or objective basis. Examples of such words are *"safek"*, meaning "doubt" (and also *"vadai"*, meaning "certain"); and *"teva"*, meaning "Nature". Doubt, of course, is not an objective Creation – nothing was Created "doubtfully", things either are or they are not; it is the subjective human experience of uncertainty which is described by the word "doubt", and that experience is purely human, not Divinely objective. (Of course certainty, too, is not an objective Torah idea; if there can be no doubt in the absolute sense, then there can be no certainty either – when things exist in the real world, they do not *certainly* exist, they simply exist. Certainty is an idea which is relevant only where doubt is a possibility.)

Nature, in the sense of an independent, self-generating or self-maintaining system, is also illusory at the deepest level, as we have seen previously. The fact that the world appears to function on its own, without obvious control from any higher Source, is certainly a human perception, and that perception is contained in the word "Nature", but the Torah does not contain such a word; in essence, the appearance of independence is inaccurate.

With this background in mind, it is instructive to search the vocabulary of a society and to identify those words which belong to this category. One may be surprised to find a number of terms which may seem indispensable and central to the thinking of a generation or even an entire culture and yet which have their origin solely in the mind of that generation or culture.

If we were to assemble a list of such terms, we could include Romance, Etiquette, Chivalry, Adventure, Entertainment, and there are many others. It must be remembered that these words convey ideas and values which are integral and important within present society. Let us study some of these in order to see whether in fact they fit our definition of ideas which contain illusory elements. We shall find that these ideas and values represent externalities; they certainly exist in the world of physicality and materialism, but in the world of essence, they are illusions.

Romance: the heady swirl of emotion which characterizes a new relationship is the hallmark of romance. There is no Hebrew word for this idea; its relative illusion is due to the fact that no real giving has yet taken place.

Hebrew certainly has a word for love, *ahava*, which at its core denotes giving. Love is the result of much genuine giving (not of taking, as is the mistaken belief in modern society), and this is an integral part of Torah. Genuine giving, giving of the self, generates love, and that love is real. But the experience of newness, the quick infatuation which is generated by superficial appearances, is illusory; it lasts only long enough to fool its victim into thinking that it will last forever, then it promptly collapses! Of course, it has a purpose, and that purpose is to inspire, to begin a relationship with energy and hope. In that sense it is a gift; but relative to genuine love it has no name.

Modern society confuses love with romance. Romance is advertised and sold as love, and of course, when romance dies, *as it must*, there is nothing left but pain and disillusionment. No-one has taught the young of this generation that real relationships are built by the very arduous work of giving, and therefore when the taking begins to wear thin, the relationship dies.

Romance comes at the beginning of a relationship, love comes later. And the height of the romantic notion is "Love at first sight", the clearest contradiction in terms imaginable. Love is not possible at first sight; there has not yet been any giving. First sight reveals the external; the insight of long experience reveals the depth.

Etiquette: the notion of etiquette comprises the system of rules of proper behavior. Correct behavior is close to the essence of Torah; but the question is: what is the source and the reason behind the behavior – is it the expression of a deep quality of good character, or is it simply superficial pedantry designed for appearances? The element within etiquette which expresses inner character is certainly valid (all superficial and even false ideas and practices *contain some truth* – that is the reason for their continued survival!); but etiquette comprises mainly rules of conduct *which are followed for the sake of the rules,* it is the rules themselves which are important. Niceties of behavior and appearance are observed *because the rules of etiquette require them.* Whether it is the arrangement of silverware on the table or the way a military officer and gentleman drinks his port, these things are essentially outer shows. Many of the practices dictated by etiquette are very important in polite society; one's good breeding and character may be judged by these observances, and yet in essence they are empty.

In Torah, there is no such thing. In Torah, every action is informed by Torah knowledge, and the action is always an expression of essence and always a training of good character (both of which in fact have a common source.) In Torah, details of dress, the manner in which one ties one's shoelaces, whether it is the man or the woman who walks first, all these are expressions of depth and builders of depth. Nothing is done for outer appearances only, and appreciation of character is based on the extent to which behavior reflects inner quality.

A certain young man who had recently entered the world of those who are finding their way back to a Torah way of life expressed his confusion to his Rabbi and teacher. He had groomed himself in good manners and gallantry in the secular world and had achieved a polished level there, and now he was attempting to learn the Torah's rules of *derech eretz,* good conduct. Should he walk first, or should his wife? Should he open the door of his vehicle for her, or was that a non-Jewish convention which has no place in Torah? And so on. The Rabbi patiently explained: "Conduct yourself with *sechel*, intelligence. Those questions depend on the circumstances: if it is raining, open her door first and let her in. But if it is hot, you enter first and open the windows!" Torah *derech eretz* expresses and trains good character; the inner depth must always be in harmony with the outer expression.

Adventure: the thrill of doing things for the sake of doing them, and particularly when danger is involved, is the basis of the world's idea of adventure. As we have remarked previously, all problematic concepts have sparks of truth and spirituality within them, and this is no exception. But the search for and preoccupation with dangerous adventure has no place in Torah. What sensible and responsible individual would go out to face danger unnecessarily? The truth is that the motivation for such behavior is the desire to experience life, *to feel alive*. One who lacks genuine life and growth experiences will seek the superficial equivalent in adventure. There are other elements involved here too, but this is not the place to analyze them. Suffice it to say that Torah has no word for this class of activity; genuine character growth is the most living experience possible and one fully engaged in it will not feel the need to leap off cliffs with a rubber rope attached to his ankles.

The message is clear. The reader can proceed to analyze the other terms and ideas dear to modern society which have no expression in Torah for a broader view of this general area. They exist on all sides; a thinking and sensitive Jew must examine all of his surroundings before accepting as valid any element of the non-Torah world in order to sift the wheat from the chaff, the inner fruit from the outer husk.

The world of esthetics is tempting; but what is its depth? Beauty in Torah is a central idea, but it must be a beauty which expresses and discovers the spiritual; then it is appropriate. When outer beauty reflects only itself, it is misapplied. Of course, it is not surprising that art's highest motto is "Art for art's sake"; this is considered to be the peak of artistic expression because it is pure, unadulterated by the ulterior or the utilitarian. But in the world of spirit, nothing is justified by itself except spirit. All else must be elevated to the spiritual, all else must be means, not ends.

II.

Torah reflects endless depth in the world. Within the physical, Torah is the point of connection with the world of spirit. It is the spark of an infinite flame, burning in a world of the finite and the superficial.

The Jewish people are likened to fire and flame, and our perennial enemies are likened to straw. The verse states *"V'haya beis Yaakov eish, u'beis Yosef lehava, u'beis Esav l'kash* – And the house of Jacob shall be fire, and the house of Joseph flame, and the house of Esau shall be straw." What exactly is the meaning of this comparison?

The Midrash gives an analogy. There was once a *pechami* – a seller of coals in the marketplace (in the ancient world, one would buy coals to light one's home fires – the *pechami* kept coals alight and glowing for sale.) A straw merchant arrived in the same marketplace and began piling up his bales of straw. After a while there was no place to move, and the *pechami* became afraid. Tons of straw were filling the market and there was no place left.

At that point, a wise man who was present spoke to the *pechami:* "What are you afraid of? When his straw gets too close to your fire, one spark from your coals will end the problem!"

This Midrash teaches a fundamental lesson about the Jewish people and the Torah in the long battle against the external forces which seek to destroy us. The Esav-nations are represented by straw: straw has only one kind of value, and that lies in quantity. A few pieces of straw are worthless; only in bulk does straw achieve value. Its worth is proportional to its mass. Those nations and cultures which oppose the spiritual, value the material, and the material has value in its mass; he who has more is wealthier. When Esav comes to meet Yaakov, he initially rejects Yaakov's gift, proclaiming his wealth: "I have much." His wealth lies in the sheer volume and mass of his possessions – "I have much." These nations would swamp the Jewish people if they could, and establish a world unfettered by moral niceties and considerations of the spiritual; in fact, they would gladly use their bulk and might to destroy Yaakov.

Yaakov, on the other hand, meets his brother's declaration of wealth with "For I have everything." Spiritual values live on a plane above mass and volume, and none of the terms relating to mass or bulk are relevant – "I have everything." Completeness is not possible in the realm of the physical, but above that realm it becomes natural.

And that is why Yaakov is likened to fire. Straw achieves value in bulk, but fire is fire no matter how little of it there is. One spark is enough to ignite a whole world of straw; and in that final and inevitable battle between the might of muscle and the light of genuine spirit, it is the small spark of real fire which will prevail. When the bales of straw, that substance which is nothing but the outer layer of the wheat within, pile up and threaten the lone coal-seller and his embers, one tiny spark from those embers will set the world ablaze and all externality and superficiality will be transformed into light.

But there is one requirement for this: the coals must retain their fire. Quantity is irrelevant, but quality is everything – if the coals harbor even one genuine spark, all will be well. But if the fire dies, then what is left is worth even less than straw. Our work is to see to it that in the Jewish heart and mind there is always a spark of genuine flame.

Chapter 8

The World of Obligation

We have examined some of the conflicts between Torah and secular values, and we have considered the idea of the structure of the natural world, its order and symmetrical organization. Let us see how these are connected; correctly understanding this subject will yield a deep insight into the point of conflict between the inner and outer worlds in the modern age.

In Torah, there is a sense of obligation. In fact, the whole Torah consists of obligation – a Jew is obliged to perform all the commandments and avoid all the Torah's prohibitions. Every word of Torah obliges. Even the verse which states that "Our days are like a passing shadow" is explained by the Sages as the *obligation* to make the most of each day.

The very first component of Torah living is to accept the bond of obligation to Hashem – the Sages illustrate this with the analogy of a nation which asks a great king for laws by which to live; the king's response is: "First, accept me as your king. Only then can I command you to fulfill specific commands." If there is no binding obligation to begin with, the commands will not be commands – just as they are voluntarily accepted now they are liable to be rejected later. Torah living consists of a basic, underlying commitment, a mindset of obligation, and following on from that basic attitude, a sense of obligation to each particular commandment – obligation from beginning to end.

"Na'aseh v'nishma – We shall do and then we shall hear (understand)." The Jewish people's acceptance of the binding nature of Torah is primary and unconditional, pledged before knowing what that acceptance will mean in practical terms. Only then do we seek to understand what it is that we have taken on. First, we sacrifice control to the Master of Creation, then we seek to build.

Torah demands allegiance, loyalty, obligation; Torah does not prescribe freedom. On the contrary, the *gemara* indicates that real freedom is to be found only in being bound by the obligations of Torah!

*   *   *

Modern society, in contrast, values freedom. The charters and constitutions of secular democracies enshrine freedom in every possible form. The idea of obligation is not popular at all in this generation. The highest value is the right to express oneself unhindered.

The idea of unfettered freedom has taken on an almost absolute value in society. Even in the Jewish world there are attempts to apply this ideology – movements which attempt to change Torah Judaism cut and or ine one obligation after another until there is no obligation left. Judaism without obligation is a contradiction in terms; but what is more insidious is the underlying misunderstanding of the human relationship with the Divine – if *I* decide what my obligations are, of course *I* am in control and those obligations are really only a thin veil for my own ego. The reliable criterion for working within Torah is: what is my motivation? Is it to define and fulfill my obligations fully without regard to the difficulty involved, or is it primarily to make life easier for myself? The former is Torah, the latter is self-serving delusion. If the primary value is the search for my real obligations, the result will be truth. If the primary value, however, is my own comfort, the result will be a distortion of reality which resembles my own inflated ego, and I will be forever trapped in a delusion of freedom. Only a slave to the truth is free.

*   *   *

Let us look more deeply into the diametrically opposed views of Torah and modern society regarding the idea of obligation. In order to do this, we shall need to understand an idea which is presented classically in the writings of Rabbi Dessler *ztz'l*, the idea of giving and taking. This idea is well-known in Torah thinking; let us summarize it briefly in order to understand its relevance to our subject of the centrality of obligation in the Torah view of life.

All relationships between people involve giving and taking. In some aspects of a relationship one party is the giver and the other receives, and in some aspects the direction of giving is the reverse. Any particular individual relates to others, and in fact to the world in general, on a continuum of giving or taking – some people are givers, some are takers.

In their depth, these two polarities represent the higher, spiritual world and the lower, material world. Giving is an attribute of the Divine; in fact, it is the primary quality of the Divine to which we can relate. Taking is foreign to the Divine; taking implies some lack, some need which is fulfilled by that which is given – obviously this is not relevant to Hashem Who lacks nothing. One who gives resembles the Divine; one who takes distances himself from his Divine image.

"*Soneh matanos yich'ye* – One who hates gifts shall live." One who loves to give is living in parallel with the Divine attributes; one who loves to receive is in conflict with that ideal. Giving is an aspect of goodness and self-sufficiency; taking is a symptom of lack and deficiency. One who loves taking, who is in the habit of taking, is training himself to live in a vacuum of lack and dependency.

Of course, sometimes receiving is actually giving – the gracious acceptance of the gift of an admirer by a great person is in fact an act of giving; in such a case it is the giver who *needs* to give, the receiver does not need the gift intrinsically but accepts it only as a favor to the giver. At root, the receiver of the gift is the real giver; what is important is the essence of the transaction and the relationship, not the transfer of a physical object. In an ideal relationship, for example an ideal marriage, both parties know how to give and also how to receive graciously; one of the deepest gifts in marriage is the opportunity one gives one's partner to be a giver!

*　　*　　*

So giving is Divine; taking is, at best, human. Now the application of this fundamental subject which sheds light on modern society (and the Jew's place in it) is as follows. In human relationships, the polarities of giving and taking can be expressed as *obligations* and *rights*. My rights are your obligations: my right to my property can be expressed as your obligation not to steal. My right to free speech is your obligation to allow me to speak freely. A worker's right to a living wage is his employer's obligation to pay that wage. It is your obligation to see to it that my rights remain intact. Every right implies an obligation; the rights of individuals are the obligations of society at large.

The important point to grasp here is that rights and obligations are interlocked; neither is meaningful without the other. Just as there can be no receiver without a giver, there can be no rights without obligations.

Now rights are parallel to taking, and obligations are parallel to giving. After all, my rights are due *to me*, I can demand them if necessary, they are *mine*. Obligations are those things which I have to do *for you*, I have to limit myself, to *give up* some of my freedom and desires in order to accommodate your rights. In guarding my rights I am a taker; in honoring my obligations I am a giver.

Of course, both rights and obligations are true and necessary. Each individual has a right to expect that which is due to him and an obligation to provide others with all that is due to them. But the essential question is: *Where is your focus?* What concerns you more – your rights or your obligations? A person who is concerned with his rights is a taker; one who is concerned with his obligations is a giver. Focusing on one's rights is focusing on the self – a constant awareness of one's needs and the desire to satisfy them. Focusing on one's obligations is focusing on others and the function of giving.

This difference of focus has far-reaching practical consequences. The Midrash describes the ideal relationship between a Jewish master and slave: the slave must work for his master as best he is able, and the master must treat his slave as a brother. Obviously, if both live up to their obligations the relationship will be productive and peaceful. But when the master focuses on *the slave's* obligation to work hard, and the slave keeps demanding that *the master* treat him better instead of working as he should – when each one forgets his obligations and thinks only of his rights – the result is war. And both are quoting the Torah! When the master reminds the slave that he is supposed to work single-mindedly and the slave reminds the master that he is supposed to treat him like a brother, both are absolutely correct – *but they are focusing on the wrong end of the deal,* and *that* is where the problems begin.

Two people in marriage, each trying to give to the other – the result is an idyllic relationship. Two people, each focusing on what *the other* owes – the result is marital strife. And paradoxically, the surest way to lose one's personal happiness is to demand it as a right from one's spouse.

Applications of this principle are to be found everywhere. In an industrial society, when employers treat employees fairly and the workers serve loyally, all is well. But when workers are concerned about their rights primarily, the natural result is that in order to protect and enforce their rights they band together in a union. The union has the power to paralyze an industry, so the employers form a national association of employers to fight the stranglehold of the union, and the result is battle.

*   *   *

Modern society is largely concerned with rights. The wording of the Constitutions of Western democracies is very revealing – they unfailingly focus on rights; in fact, they are often little more than a detailed enumeration of the rights of the individuals in that particular society. The highest code of such societies is their Bill of Rights.

In striking contrast is the Torah, the Jewish Constitution. *The Torah never mentions rights,* only obligations! Nowhere does the Torah speak of an individual's right to his property; only his obligation not to steal. No mention of a right to life or liberty; only stringent admonitions not to kill or interfere with the liberty of one's fellow. Not even a cursory mention of one's right to happiness, dignity, physical well-being or sustenance; only strong reminders of the duty to provide others with these. And so on.

Of course rights exist; of course they are important. The Oral Law is full of discussions of individual's rights. But the point is that the focus is everything. In a perfect society, which is the inevitable result of meticulous Torah observance, individuals consider and live up to their obligations. When each person watches his obligations carefully, *the rights take care of themselves.* If no-one steals, everyone's right to property is assured automatically. If no-one interferes with anyone, everyone's freedom is the result. When people are givers, happiness results. When everyone is giving, everyone receives.

A society which enshrines rights is a society which develops takers. A society which focuses on obligations develops givers. The specific details of a political system are far less important than this basic idea; in fact, *no* political system will work when the individuals who comprise that system are inherently takers – they will always be trying to take what they can from the system, and usually feel that they are not getting enough. Conversely, almost any political system will work admirably when its members are careful to contribute at least as much as they receive.

The great secret of political and social stability is that the *individuals* within a system must inherently be givers. The Torah insists on this; a child raised in a Torah environment is a child who is trained to be conscious of his obligations. Such a member of society can be relied upon, even when no-one is watching!

Of course, there is a very important condition which must apply before any individual can give fully and unconditionally in society: everyone else must be so disposed too! If an individual tries to live up to his obligations with no regard to his rights in a society of takers, that individual will be swallowed alive. It is therefore the aim of Torah education to produce an individual who is intrinsically a giver, but who knows how to protect himself from the unscrupulous when that is necessary.

Being a full-hearted giver does not mean being naive about the realities of modern society; Torah openly discusses the wiles and duplicity of the evil and teaches appropriate self-defence. When Yaakov lives with Lavan who is a swindler and a cheat, Yaakov has to subdue his inner core of pure giving and deal with Lavan on his own terms in order to survive and succeed; his greatness, however, is that it leaves him inwardly untainted. In the privacy of the Jewish heart and family, pure giving is the appropriate mode; in a murderous and perverse environment, self-defence is necessary – but it must never affect the core.

*   *   *

Modern society seeks freedom from obligation. One of the Torah predictions of the state of affairs which will exist in the pre-Messianic age states: "The face of the generation will be like the face of the dog." One of the layers of meaning in this statement is this: a dog runs ahead of its master but looks back to see which path the master will take. The dog appears to be leading but in fact it is taking direction from its master – when the master turns, the dog doubles back and then again runs ahead down the new road which the master has chosen. The dog is always ahead, but in reality it is always following. Such will be the behavior of the pre-Messianic generation: its leaders will appear to be leading but in fact they will be lackeys of the populace, following the will of the masses. They will stand at the head of nations and strut and pose as if they determine direction, but in reality they will always be looking to the people for that direction.

It may come as a surprise to those raised in the Western liberal tradition, but this is an accurate description of democracies. Modern democracy, the pride of the Western liberal outlook, functions exactly as predicted. The leaders appear to lead, but in fact they are entirely dependent on the populace for their leadership. Their entire aim is to satisfy the wishes of the electorate – after all, if they do not, they will not be elected. They enjoy the pomp and state of kings, but their authority is entirely in the hands of the masses, those who control by means of their vote.

The electorate in this age is not interested in obligations, only in rights, and they therefore do not accept the binding leadership of their leaders but control their leaders entirely. The leaders are not leaders at all.

Leaders in modern democratic systems openly maneuver for votes. Positions are taken more for their likely popularity than for their intrinsic morality. Modern politicians openly admit that they seek power – politics is the battle for the position of leadership and the battle to maintain power once it is achieved. These aims are open, unashamedly admitted. Surely leadership should be centered around concern for the people – the very last individual who should be considered for power is the one who wants it! Secular leadership is taking, not giving, and all too often such leaders are ready to kill for their power.

In Torah, leadership, like all of Torah, is obligation, not privilege. Torah leaders throughout history have been chosen for their humility and their very desire *not to be leaders!* Moshe argues vehemently with Hashem that he is not fit for leadership – Hashem eventually forces it upon him. David is called in from tending his father's sheep to be anointed. Many of the prophets are sent on their missions under severe duress. The Elders who are leaders of the Jewish people in the desert are chosen because while in Egypt they accepted the beatings meted out by the Egyptians in order to spare their Jewish charges – the criterion for Jewish leadership is the willingness to *suffer* for the people, not the desire for the glory of office! Many Jewish leaders were shepherds for years before they were chosen to lead; tending the flock, protecting the sheep from predators and the elements is a fitting preparation for leadership, not years spent in the cut-and-thrust of the political arena.

In depth, there is very little control when a society's outlook is based on unlimited freedom. The leaders' authority is hollow; the laws of society are not deeply binding: they are simply the expression of the will of the people – the people decide what will be law, and when a particular set of laws no longer appeals to a society, new laws are voted into effect and a new reality is established. The laws are not absolute, they are the products of the understanding and the attitudes of the populace – in the final analysis, really only the whims of a generation.

A law which binds me only as long as I allow it to do so is not binding at all. A society which decides its own limitations from within has no limitations – they will shift and change as the desires of the generation drift. The will of the people is primary, the law comes second.

In Torah, the opposite applies. As it has been beautifully and succinctly stated: in a democracy, the people make the law; in Torah, the Law makes the people.

*   *   *

Let us look more deeply into the idea of giving and taking. Taking is related to the present – when I take, I have what I want now. Giving is an investment in the future – when I give, apart from the pleasure of giving, I may not see the effects for a long time; in fact, all I may experience now is the sacrifice of that which I am giving away. A Jewish life is invested in the future; that is the meaning of *emuna*, faith. I do what I must because it is correct, because I am obliged; I am not looking for an immediate result. The focus on giving and obligation is a focus on another time and another world. Just as the farmer plants seeds and tends them while the crop is yet a season distant, so too the person of faith plants in this world and knows that in another time and another season the fruits will result.

This is the path of maturity; but the immature mind is always seeking a "quick fix", immediate gratification. It is sobering to note that our generation is intent on "quick fixes". Things that demand time and patience are not popular. That which is not "instant" does not sell. A generation ago a simple cup of tea involved many steps – one first heated a teapot, then waited long minutes for the leaves to draw; the cup was heated before the tea was poured, and it had to be strained while being poured. Who brews tea now? Machines are advertised as superior because they perform millions of functions in milliseconds – not long ago the same functions took *years* to be done; these are soon considered slow because a newer model performs more in nanoseconds, and patience is a thing of the past.

The need for instant gratification is a symptom of immaturity, an infantile trait, and it stems in depth from the focus on self and the taking which serves that self. The long-forgotten art of patience is an excellent training for maturity and true depth, and it is a prerequisite for building a personality whose natural mode is giving.

*   *   *

There is another depth in the idea of obligation. *"Gadol ha'metsuveh v'oseh... –* Greater is he who is commanded and does..."* We have a principle that one who does because he is commanded is greater than one who acts spontaneously. This is counter-intuitive; surely spontaneity is greater? Surely if an action is generated within myself it is greater than an action performed because I am obliged from without?

One of the classic answers to this question is that when one is commanded to act, one is immediately confronted by resistance – one's own *yetzer ha'ra*, or lower self, steps in and says "Don't tell me what to do!" The ego, the "I", that deep root of the personality (and its spiritual core), wishes to assert itself, refuses to be subdued. Therefore, in order to fulfill a command one must overcome this inner resistance, and in doing so lies the secret of inner growth. Self-control is at the heart of all personal growth, and it is developed by the discipline required to obey. However, when one acts spontaneously there is no resistance to overcome and the action is relatively easy; it is not intrinsically an exercise in self-control and therefore has relatively little growth potential.

But there is more here than meets the eye. When one acts spontaneously, motivated only by that which arises within one's own consciousness, one is expressing oneself. That may be a great thing, but it can never be greater than the individual who is performing the act. At best, the act will be a full and true expression of the one who performs it. But when one fulfills a Divine command one is expressing the Divine! The person who acts in fulfilling a commandment is no less than a partner with the Divine; that person has locked into the infinite dimension and reveals in the world what the Divine Source of that action intends to reveal. The word *mitzva* is based on a root meaning "together", partners.

"Gadol ha'metsuveh..." – far greater is the one who acts because he is commanded!

The secret depth here is that in overcoming the private, limited self, *because* one overcomes that individual self, one arrives at a greater Self, one merits a closeness with the Source of reality.

*   *   *

Let us return to our starting point: obligation. What is the connection between a sense of obligation and the theme of structure and symmetry which we have studied?

The vessel in the personality which holds the sense of obligation is an ordered mind. A sense of structure, an organized framework, is a requirement for a mindset of obligation. A disorganized, disintegrated personality does not sense being obliged. Let us attempt to explain why this is so at root.

As we have seen, obligation means limitations. If I live according to my obligations, I must do certain things and I must not do others. A specific set of limitations is imposed on my behavior. *Structure also means limitations* – a structured form has a specific shape; an organized structure means that the form has limitations, it is *obliged* by the rules of symmetry and balance. The parts cannot be disposed any way they may fall – there are demands to be met, harmonies to be maintained.

This is the deep connection between structure and obligation. Only a mind which is organized, structured, can sense the order of a system of obligation.

Deeper yet, only such a mind can grasp the essence of truth. The truth is ultimately limited – there are many false answers to any particular problem, infinitely many. But the truth is limited; it derives from the world of Oneness, its nature is to be one. There are many falsehoods but only one truth. In this, truth is the ultimate constraint, and in this, too, truth is the ultimate freedom. The disorganized mind wanders in falsehoods. The organized, structured mind pursues paths that are true and *only* paths that are true. Such a mind perceives an obligation to the truth. Only a slave to the truth is free.

Chapter 9

Intimacy and Morality

To understand the relationship between higher and lower worlds one must understand the nature of the bond between man and woman. It is here, perhaps more than anywhere else, that obligation and loyalty are intrinsic and essential. The breakdown which the modern world is experiencing in the area of intimacy between man and woman plays a pivotal role in the broader picture of societal problems which beset this age.

What is the nature of this intimacy and why does it occupy such a prominent part of the human psyche? Why is so much of society's activity and consciousness focused on this aspect of human functioning? The natural attraction of this area is not due to the drive for pleasure alone – there are many pleasures of the body, yet we do not find society preoccupied with any of them in a way even vaguely comparable with its preoccupation with this subject. The libraries of the world are filled with books which relate to it in one way or another, and a cursory look at the world of advertising will show that virtually everything which can tempt man is promoted by being linked to the temptation of the male-female relationship. That is the center; all else is secondary. Why must this be so?

*   *   *

In this area lie deep secrets. The truth is that in the relationship between man and woman is reflected the inner connection between higher and lower worlds, between the Divine source-dimension and the physical world, and between Hashem and the Jewish people.

If one wishes to understand the spiritual depth of this subject, one must approach it by studying and understanding its revealed manifestation; in analyzing the experience of male and female interaction sensitively and accurately one will find all the insight necessary to perceive the root. What exactly is the nature of this most potent and fascinating human experience? What does it contain that so captivates the mind and heart? Why in fact does it exert so powerful an attraction that many students of human nature claim that it is the central element in all human motivation?

The answer is that in the intimate depth of this relationship is contained a sensation of end-point, of having arrived, of having no place else to go and in fact no need to go anywhere else at all. The sensation at the root of human consciousness which is generated here is that a process has reached its goal; all movement finally stops here, comes to rest in the deepest sense possible. The pleasure which can be felt here is not simply that of earthy sensibility, of nerve endings and animal experience; these elements are immeasurably amplified by a consciousness of *tachlis*, of purpose achieved, of coming home most intensely. This is not a function perceived as process or preparation, it is not fulfilled with a sense of future; rather, past and future melt away in a present so intense that it seems to swell to infinite proportions.

Why is this so? What cosmic energy underlies this interaction? The answer is that here lies the microcosm, the human-sized experience of all *tachlis*, of worlds coming together, of process meeting result, of body and soul joining at root, of life itself. Here the sower and the reaper meet, here the spiritual infuses the physical with its energy. Here is the this-worldly image of the supernal meeting of the Divine with the Universe and of Hashem with His people. Here lies the sensation of transition from this world to the next, where all process becomes result, where all the pain of work and waiting gives way to the exhilaration of unity with the Purpose of life. Is it any wonder that this area, when sensitively and spiritually entered, has the power to build a depth of relationship which is indescribable, and is it any wonder that this is where life is generated?

*   *   *

And is it any wonder that a perverse and non-spiritual generation profanes this area above all else? If the animal is loosed in this sacred zone, if human depth and sublime understanding are eliminated from this fragile zone of wonder, if the unique privacy and modesty which belong here are damaged, then there is no spiritual in the world of flesh and there can be no possibility of elevating the physical.

In Torah we find this subject brought to the fore in the life and personality of Yosef. In the deeper wisdom Yosef represents the quality of *yesod*, "Foundation", which is the area of covenant between male and female. Yosef is referred to as *Yosef ha'Tzaddik*, Yosef the Righteous; the essential quality indicated by the term *tzaddik* is that of doing exactly what must be done without the slightest straying or deficiency. Yosef was the one who resisted the advances of his master's wife in superhuman fashion, conquering the supreme temptation she offered for an extended period of time while he was yet a youth. Yosef represents absolute control of the sensuality of the male-female relationship, absolute application of this energy to a proper purpose with no straying.

In a certain sense, Yosef is one of the forefathers of the Jewish people. Unlike the other sons of Yaakov Avinu who each became a Tribe of Israel, Yosef is represented by two Tribes – his sons Ephraim and Menashe; Yosef is more of a father than a son. Fatherhood is the expression of his essential quality. And Yosef's fatherhood is entirely loyal, his energy as a father within the Jewish people is directed only where it is appropriate, rejecting the temptation of illicit application of his maleness entirely. In fact, his two sons represent these two respective facets of his depth: "Ephraim" is connected with the root meaning "fruit" – he is the pure fruit borne of a pure tree; and "Menashe" derives from a root which indicates maintaining a distance, keeping away, in this case from that which is improper and impure.

And Yosef, as a father, instilled this strength of control into his progeny and the entire Jewish people – as a result of his supernal self-control, say the Sages, the entire Jewish nation inherited the ability to remain above temptation in this area: during hundreds of years of slavery in Egypt the Jews remained untainted by immorality, untainted by that which was the norm in Egyptian society, untainted despite being a downtrodden slave people who had not yet received the Torah. And that Jewish distaste for sensual immorality persisted unweakened for millennia.

*   *   *

In the battle to be truly human, in the quest for transcendence within the world, this is the fulcrum; here the battle is pitched. The alternatives are clear and compelling – the abandon of animal instinct which senses only the present, or that deep and private sense of investment in a relationship built for eternity.

Let us probe more deeply into this mystery: what is the meaning of the potency of human experience compressed into this zone? Why is there this sense of timelessness and ultimate "having arrived" inherent in this particular interaction?

The secret here is startling in its depth: the source of all that is contained in the intimacy between man and woman in this world is in fact the nature of existence in the world to come. The ecstasy of the next world, clumsy though our grasp of it may be, is the bond between the clarified and elevated human soul and the Creator. In that ineffable relationship is contained the ultimate sensation, the knowledge, of having arrived. In that state of togetherness, ultimately and absolutely, there is no other place to go. There, the human *neshama* could not possibly conceive of moving away. There, in the deepest sense possible, time and motion stretch into the infinite meshing of the *neshama* with its Source at a cosmic intensity. There, differentiation becomes Unity, two become One in essence. And there, in the most fundamental sense, life is conceived.

All experience in this world reflects its source in the higher experience. When that higher experience is the ultimate and eternal relationship between the Creator and the human soul, the parallel experience in this world which it generates must be exceptionally potent and ecstatic.

*   *   *

If we look deeper in an attempt to define more closely the nature of the experience of a *neshama* in the next world, we note that a central feature of existence in the next world is the lack of obligation. This world is built for work, but the essence of the dimension which we call the next world is entirely reward. In that blissful state there is no work to be done; only the fruits of a lifetime's work to be enjoyed. The sensation is that of *p'tur*, of being exempt from all work and all bondage. The experience is of ultimate freedom. In fact, when a person leaves this world, the expression we use for that transition indicates exactly the change from work to reward: we say the person is *niftar* – literally "exempt", free of *mitzvos* and all obligation.

In this-worldly terms, the parallel to that ultimate experience of being exempt is the freedom one feels at those moments of being divested of responsibility, those moments of ending a phase of work or obligation. The heady sense of freedom enjoyed at the start of a vacation, at the moment when the doors of the workplace are closed and locked; at the moment when the final school-bell rings and the unfettered weekend beckons; when a person stretches out on a beach with no appointments to keep and no responsibilities to fulfill; these are microcosms of the experience of a state in which existence is justified in its own terms, in fact needs no justification at all. These are moments of existence during which time seems to halt, moments during which one feels richly that one is not travelling but that one has arrived.

And the moments during which the feeling of having arrived at a destination from which further movement is irrelevant, impossible, most intensely are those moments during which man and woman find each other most intensely. There, the experience is of life itself. And therein lies the danger of this zone of intensity: if it is used responsibly, loyally, used only with the intention to build, to sanctify, to bond in a relationship of pure obligation, then it is truly justified. Paradoxically, this experience of freedom must be used in bondage; bondage to a spouse, bondage to purpose and elevation. If this experience is used as an escape from the world of building, from the world of work, then it is entirely out of place because this world is not meant for freedom from growth and obligation; that is the province of the world to come and it cannot be entered here. One who seeks to be free here, to be exempt here, must forfeit the achievements which this world is designed to build.

The Jew does not seek escape or exemption. The sweetness of this world and all its experiences lies in savoring that foretaste of the freedom of the next world *in the very acts of fulfilling obligations* in this world; in truth, those acts are the stuff of eternal freedom. When performed in loyalty, in deep commitment to the deepest purpose, those acts of bondage are acts of building freedom and they resonate with the sensation of real and lasting freedom.

*   *   *

In human experience there is another activity which provides a rich sense of that which is done entirely for its own sake, and that is the unique activity that we call a game. The idea of a game is essentially an activity which is enjoyed simply for the sake of the enjoyment it provides. Of course, games may be played for a variety of purposes, but if one examines this subject carefully one finds that at the heart of the experience of play lies the pleasure of an activity that leads nowhere; a pure game is played for no end outside of the game itself. And that is the secret of the pleasure inherent in a game: while I am engrossed in this game, regardless of the specific nature of the game, I am divorced from the world of my obligations; I am in a state of being in which my goal lies within the activity itself, I am not striving towards a point in the future, I am not looking beyond the present at all.

A game may consist of entirely trivial actions and processes and yet be a delicious experience – surely this is a strange phenomenon? But on the contrary, that is exactly the secret: because there is nothing inherently meaningful in the moves and actions of the game, there precisely lies its escape. Within a game is a zone of wonder, a zone isolated from the bonds and pressures of the reality of a life which is entirely obligation and work; but the point to grasp is that the isolation from the world of work is not a simple escape of forgetfulness or unconsciousness akin to the experience of rest; it is precisely the nature of a game itself which intrinsically and deeply holds the domain of that escape.

If one understands this idea well it will be no surprise to discover that in the deeper sources the higher world is described as a world of play. The *gemara* states that Hashem "plays" with the Torah (and that He "plays" with the Leviathan – a subject which needs elucidation in its own right). These statements sound strange in the extreme; but if one remembers that Torah *always* deals with essence and *never* with the superficial, one will begin to understand: "playing" in essence means *doing that which is an end in itself*, that which needs no justification outside of itself, that which leads nowhere other than to its own center. Torah is the core and essence of existence, in depth it does not lead outwards, rather, all else leads to it. The world was created for Torah, it is the end-point and Hashem's original and deepest purpose, and therefore His engaging the Torah *must* be described in terms of ultimate *tachlis*, ultimate purpose. He is not using the Torah for a purpose outside of itself, so to speak, but rather all of existence finds its meaning entirely within Torah.

Nothing could be clearer than the meaning of the word itself: in Hebrew, the word for "play", that word which is used for Hashem's ineffable interaction with His Torah, is *sha'ashua*. This is a fascinating word in Hebrew: it is comprised of two similar components, the root שע *sha* duplicated. This root means "to turn towards", as we find in Bereishis (Genesis) *"Va'yisha Hashem* – And Hashem turned towards..."; and *"lo sha'a* – He did not turn towards..." The double expression of this root in the word *sha'ashua* means quite literally "turning towards the turning towards"! Is this not exactly the idea of a game – the idea of movement towards and within itself entirely?

And that is the source of the happiness and the laughter generated by play in the lower world of human action. The Hebrew words for "laughter" and for "play" are closely related – *tz'chok* and *s'chok*; and it should be no surprise at all that the word used for intimacy between man and wife in Torah is this very word: *"V'hinei Yitzchak m'tzachek es Rivka ishto* – And Yitzchak was causing Rivka his wife to laugh"; explained by the commentaries (and as apparent from the context) as marital intimacy. There are no empty euphemisms in Torah; the delicate and pure language of Torah is always exact.

* * *

The next world can be considered as the ultimate experience of play; the ecstasy of pure existence in and of itself. And the intimate bond between Hashem and the human *neshama* in that world is well described in the same terms. The sweetness of pure intimacy, intimacy informed by spirituality, is the sweetness of making pure fruit in the most real sense.

And it is precisely because real fruit is produced in this area, and therefore because the world depends on this area for the generation of human life itself, that the Creator has invested it with singular sweetness – He has spread His honey thickest here as both a revelation of secret depth and as motivation.

The great Reb Yerucham used to say that here the honey is thick because here the purpose is most important – the analogy he would give is that of the mother who smears honey on bread so that her child will eat. The mother is more interested in the bread than the honey – she wants the child to eat bread, so she is prepared to make it attractive with honey. The child, however, is interested in the honey – bread alone would not tempt him – and he is prepared to eat the bread in order to taste the honey.

Hashem gives us the sweetness of honey here because He is interested in the real fruits of the male-female relationship – the bringing down of *neshamos* into the world, and the love and loyalty which should be built in human marriage. When the bread is coated with honey, it is sweet and the purpose is achieved.

But a *shlegter kind*, a bad child, *licks off the honey and discards the bread*. A generation which defeats the purpose of this most sacred and purposefully designed area of human functioning, seeking to enjoy its honey while rejecting its responsibility, is no better (and perhaps a lot worse) than an immature child who throws his mother's kindness and wisdom back in her face. Honey eaten alone is sweet only for a while; it soon becomes unbearable. Tampering with the sweetest dimension of the human experience in a selfish attempt to divest it of its wholesome purpose must lead to destruction; first, destruction of itself, and later, destruction of the fabric of self, family and society.

The Torah prescription is simply to eat the bread with the honey. Escape from obligation, escape from the deep and correct relationship which should exist between man and woman, is escape from the spiritual. The Jew's pathway is clear: to take that experience which naturally takes one out of obligation and to use it entirely in obligation. It is to take the function of escape from obligation, of free and unbonded abandon, and to harness exactly that function to the deepest obligation possible. That is the way: to give this gift of Hashem back as a gift; that is the only way to earn it as the gift of eternal freedom in reality.

Chapter 10

Speech, Prophecy and Wasting Words

I.

There are two expressions of the theme of *bris*, covenant, in the body: the *bris ha'ma'or* – circumcision, and the *bris ha'lashon* – the covenant of the tongue. Both are creative, both are energies of connection, and both must be used carefully and loyally. We have studied some of the meaning of the former; let us now look at the latter, the world of speech.

The function of speech parallels the function of reproduction – in the lower world of the body, the output is offspring, the physical being of a child. In the higher world of the head, the output is words. Just as children are an outward expression of the body of the parent, so too words are the outward expression of the mind of the speaker.

Words are seminal; when correctly used they are a deep revelation of their source in the consciousness of the one who speaks them, and their energy is powerful enough to build a deep connection between the speaker and the one who listens. With the body one forms children; with the power of communication one creates *talmidim* – students, spiritual offspring. *"Ha'nefesh asher asu b'Charan* – the souls which they made in Charan"*, states the verse; in fact, this reference is not to children whom Avraham and Sarah brought into the world, as it may seem at first glance, but to the people whom they taught and influenced.

"Making souls" in the spiritual sense is a more significant creative act than its physical counterpart of bringing children into the physical world; in some ways the connection between Torah teacher and *talmid* is closer than between father and son, as the *halacha* states; the father brings the son into this world, but the Rebbe (teacher) brings him into the next world.

The Zohar states that wasting Torah words, attempting to teach one who is not fit to be a *talmid*, is similar to the sin of wasting the power of intimacy. Both constitute a wasteful spilling of deeply creative energy.

*   *   *

Speech is the world of connection. Understood simply, speech connects the speaker and the listener. A relationship can develop, can flourish, because deep communication is possible by means of speech. In Torah, "speaking" is sometimes used as a euphemism for intimacy ("They saw her speaking with one...") This is not a usage borrowed from a distance; the parallel is intrinsic.

At a deeper level, speech represents the connection between higher and lower worlds. Speech is the mechanism by which an abstract idea which exists only in the higher dimension of thought can be brought down into the material world: when I speak, I transform ideas into the physical medium of sound, which is tangible enough for you to hear with the physical tools of hearing. Of course, you immediately transform my words back into their abstract state of ideas in your own mind. We have used the physical medium of speech to transmit non-physical ideas; we have connected the abstract with the material.

*   *   *

In the physical structure of the body, there is a manifestation of this idea of connection which is inherent in the power of speech. It is no accident that the voice is produced in the neck. Voice is the root of speech, the power of connecting worlds; the neck is that part of the human form which connects head and body, the higher and lower domains. The body always reflects its spiritual roots.

This parallel goes further. If we look more closely, we note that the voice is produced in the throat, which is at the front of the neck. The deeper tradition states that the front of a structure represents its positive power; the back represents its lower, or faller., aspect. The front of the body in general represents positivity – the face is a feature of the front, not the back. Human relationship is possible when people face each other and difficult when they turn their backs. The back is blind, impersonal, and it is the location of offensive excretion. These things are all exquisitely specific features of the human pattern.

Now we note that the front of the neck contains the organ of voice production; the back of the neck is silent. In fact, the deeper wisdom states that the front of the neck, or throat, is identified with Moshe Rabbenu – after all, Moshe is the voice of Torah; Hashem speaks through Moshe's throat. "The Divine Presence speaks from Moshe's throat." The same sources state that Moshe's arch-enemy, Pharaoh, is represented by the back of the neck – he is the one who strives for the opposite of that which Moshe Rabbenu wishes to achieve; Pharaoh's goal is to keep the Divine voice out of the world, to silence the voice of the spiritual. Moshe Rabbenu's task is to achieve connection, the ultimate connection of spiritual and physical worlds; Pharaoh's work is to separate those worlds. Arch-enemies indeed. And the letters of the word פרעה "Pharaoh", when reversed, spell העורף "ha'oref", the back of the neck!

*　　*　　*

Prophecy is a higher form of speech. When a prophet speaks, a direct connection is formed between higher and lower worlds. Human speech reveals the thoughts and intentions of the speaker, prophecy reveals the thoughts and intentions of the Divine.

Divine speech is ultimately potent i 1 its creativity. The expression used for speech is *niv s'fa'sa jim* – "fruit of the lips"; the prophet states that Hashem's word always bears fruit – "For as the rain... descends from the Heavens and shall not return there until it has caused the land to flourish and it has given birth and caused to sprout, and given seed to the sower... *So shall be My word...*"

*　　*　　*

Speech reveals the hidden, makes it manifest. In truth, all human action does this; any meaningful action reveals in the world what was the intention of the one who performs that action. In fact, the root *dabar*, meaning speech, more literally indicates any translation of intention into action; it is an expression of *hanhaga*, control or commanding action, as in *"dabar echad l'dor* – one leader of a generation", or *"yad'ber amim tachtenu* – He shall bring nations under our control." Human action reveals the human mind, the structure and processes of the world reveal the Divine Mind; all human action is a form of speech, and all of the world is a form of Divine speech.

With this idea in mind, the evil of lies can be understood. If the proper function of speech is to reveal the hidden world, then the evil of *sheker*, falsehood, is that it uses the very tool which is designed and created to reveal in such a way that it hides. Truth is the accurate revelation of that which is hidden; lies present an external version which betrays the depth. When the outer representation has no basis in the inner reality, that outer picture is treacherous. The immorality of lies is akin to the immorality of the body – each is a use of the physical or external in disloyalty to the spiritual or inner dimension.

II.

Perhaps we can now begin to understand the severity of sins of speech in Torah. Speech is the basic tool of Creation and revelation, as we have noted, and the ability to speak is the hallmark of the human. Misuse of this central gift is particularly devastating – the first sin ever committed was brought about by improper speech: the serpent's devious words to the unsuspecting Chava (Eve). In that immoral and treacherous temptation lay all the danger that misused speech can hold.

There is an aspect of the misuse of speech which needs special study: wasting words. There is a particular problem in wasting words, even when the words spoken are not false or intrinsically sinful. In general, this is part of the problem of wasting any human resource: any time or effort wasted in a human life is wastage of that life itself and therefore a very serious matter. But wasted words, *d'varim b'telim*, are particularly problematic.

A lie presents a false picture of that which is hidden within, it betrays the inner dimension. *D'varim b'telim*, wasted and meaningless words, present a picture of that which has no inner dimension, and this is no less a betrayal. Words are given in order to reveal meaning, to clothe a deeper reality; empty nonsense betrays the very fact that there is a depth at all.

The Vilna Gaon states that the consequence of wasted words is a particular suffering in the next world: *kaf ha'kela*, the "cup of the slingshot"; a *neshama* which must endure that particular suffering as a result of wasting words experiences the sensation of being flung from one place to another, but before arriving at the destination is flung yet again in another direction, and so on. The Gaon says that for *every empty statement* a person must be flung from one end of the world to the other. There is an experience of constant travelling towards a goal, but never arriving – this is the reality generated by a life which used the tools of human growth for nothing other than their own sake, a life which moved through the world but wasted its creative energies.

Such a life consists of talking constantly but not saying anything; the version of such a life which is reflected in the next world, the world of reality, is the experience of moving but not arriving. To speak and create is to live in the Divine image; to speak without creating is to negate that image.

The world is full of empty words. The nature of modern media is such that there is virtually no limit to the amount of words which are spewed out constantly, and our society is inundated with talk. But it seems that the more words that are poured out, the less meaning they convey. We have plenty of words, but very little communication.

*   *   *

One of the mysteries of the sin of wasting words is why it feels so good: why do people relish spending hours talking nonsense? It is a particular feature of human interaction that there is intense pleasure in speaking to an acquaintance or in a group of people for long periods even when no important or relevant subject is discussed. People often get together for no purpose other than to chat. If one cares to analyze the flow of such conversations one will find that the topics discussed range widely and wildly with almost no logical connection between them other than mere association of ideas – one topic leads to another, some detail of that topic suggests another topic, the discussion veers in that direction for a while, and so on. Very often one cannot even trace the course of the discussion or remember what was covered. And yet – the experience was thoroughly enjoyed by all.

It is sobering to note that a large proportion of human conversation, perhaps the major part, belongs to this category of idle and directionless speech. One has only to listen to a party of people relaxing over dinner or socializing in some other context to be struck by the random and irrelevant nature of the talk. And again, it is pleasurable. If nothing in the make-up of the psyche is accidental, why is this so?

In order to understand this phenomenon we shall have to study a particular depth of human motivation. The *gemara* states that *Anshei Knesses Ha'gdola*, the Men of the Great Assembly, annulled the human drive for idolatry. They reckoned that due to the relative descent of the generations in spiritual power, the ordeal provided by the temptation to idolatry was greater than the reward to be earned in overcoming it. Since it offered too dangerous a test, they decided to work for its obliteration, and they successfully exorcised it from the human psyche. From that time on, people do not have a natural and intrinsic drive to worship idols.

But the very act of abolishing the drive to idolatry also abolished prophecy. That generation was the last to experience prophecy; in fact, Chaggai, Zecharia and Malachi were the last three prophets and they were members of that great convocation of Sages and prophets. What is the connection between idolatry and prophecy? Why must they stand or fall together?

The answer is that both of these ideas relate to transcendence. The human mind and *neshama* long to transcend the bounds of the finite and physical, and essentially, such transcendence is possible. At a high enough level of human preparation and purity, prophecy is the result. In prophecy, the *neshama* breaks through into a transcendent realm, breaks through into a zone outside of the self and closer to that of the Creator, and the experience is of a magnitude that is impossible for us to understand.

But there is a false channel for transcendence, too. That is the idea of idolatry; the desire to annul the self in an experience of merging with a greater reality can be misdirected to idolatrous ends. Idolatry provides an opportunity for going beyond the self; it provides a sense of transcendence, but of course in a false and misguided way. In fact, in its impure heart, idolatry is really worship of the self, but its guise is worship of that which is above.

Prophecy is a pathway, a channel, to reach above the self. Idolatry is a false pathway to reach above, a misguided application of the faculty of relating to that which is above the human realm. And that is why they both inhabit the same zone within human consciousness and motivation – the very pinnacle of the mind, the point at which consciousness can transcend into the superconscious, is that faculty which is activated in prophecy and betrayed in idolatry.

And that is why they stand or fall together. If that most powerful drive, the drive to connect with the Divine in prophecy, is removed, then the temptation to worship a false version of holiness is removed too. And the reason is that they are one and the same faculty in the mind. There is no intrinsic good or bad in the human form, only energies which are more or less powerful; good and bad lie solely in the application of those energies. If there is an energy directed at rising above the finite, at transcending, then that energy will be the stuff of prophecy, and of necessity it will be the stuff of the drive to idolatry. If prophecy goes, the temptation to idolatry will be deflated too.

What has happened is that the organ, the faculty of the mind which is able to reach above itself has been excised, and all its functions must disappear as a result. If one removes an organ of the body surgically, all of its functions are lost – one cannot expect some functions of the liver to remain intact in the body if the liver has been removed, and similarly, when the Men of the Great Assembly removed the craving for idolatry from the human heart, they were simultaneously removing prophecy from the realm of human attainment. What was in fact removed was not idolatry or prophecy in themselves, but rather the mental and spiritual faculty which spawns them. When that faculty was removed, its functions disappeared.

Now the fascinating question is: when a part of the mind is thus weakened or removed, what remains in its place? And the answer is: nothing. But let us understand: we are discussing the highest faculty, the point of origin of the mind, the point of origin of consciousness. This point represents the highest drive imaginable, the drive for reaching up, the drive for the ecstasy of bonding with the Creator. And when that point is emptied, what is left is *a drive for nothing at all*. The drive to move out and beyond has become *a drive to be where one is* and not to progress. The space remains, that area of the psyche remains, the drive remains; but instead of being geared to reaching up and on, it remains as a drive to be involved in movement which does not have to go anywhere. The pleasure of being able to transcend has become the pleasure of being in a place which is an end in itself. Talking about nothing, using the deepest and most creative of human faculties for nothing other than its own sake, is the result.

When the real transcendence of prophecy was possible, a sane individual would not have enjoyed talking nonsense, talking or working or moving without the achievement of tangible progress; nothing could have been more frustrating. But now that we have a zone of emptiness where the zone of transition to a higher state once was, we enjoy simply using our tools of progress to go nowhere.

* * *

There is another depth here, though. In order to better understand what we have studied, our discussion of intimacy and its sensation of "having arrived" must be remembered. We studied the idea of those activities, such as games, which have as their core the experience of *p'tur*, of total exemption from obligation and growth; those activities which yield pleasure specifically because they constitute a "time-out" from the bonds of obligation, from the work of moving and building. In the world of *mitzvos*, Shabbos is the representation of this dimension – on Shabbos, we do not build the world, we desist from all actions of building in the physical. Shabbos is a state of being, not becoming; of having arrived, not travelling; and Shabbos holds the key to the next world, that ultimate state of being and of having arrived.

Talking for the sake of talking, interacting with others for the sake of the interaction itself, holds this pleasure potently. The root of the mind is the faculty of transcendence which is now a faculty of "end-in-itself", and of course it is this same area which is the gateway to the pleasure of the next world, that state of being in which there is genuinely no other place to go. When we experience that which makes us feel that we wish we could remain in this state permanently, forever freeze this moment of pleasure which holds no obligation, forever feel this freedom, we are resonating with the highest mode of the human soul, an echo of the world to come.

And that is part of the understanding of the universal and peculiar human motivation to speak endlessly about that which is utterly meaningless. But the real obligation here is not to yield to that temptation which is both utterly frivolous and yet very high indeed. Our obligation is to make every word count. Each word is precious, each word is a spark of the fire of one's depth which can be used to ignite endless fires of life and spirit, and using each word thus is the avenue to that higher world which is all light.

Chapter 11

Clouded Lens, Clear Lens

W e have considered prophecy as the connection between worlds, as the channel through which the source dimension is revealed. Prophecy itself has various levels – the lens of prophetic revelation may be clear or unclear. Let us attempt to look into an aspect of the world of prophecy and its root.

In that classic formulation of Jewish belief, the Thirteen *Ikkarim*, or Fundamentals, the Rambam includes the principle of prophecy. (The wording of these Fundamentals may not be the Rambam's own, but their essence follows his formulation.) The sixth Fundamental states: "I believe... that all the words of the prophets are true." This is one of the Fundamentals because without the principle of prophecy there can be no direct link with the Source. It is through prophecy that we are aware of Hashem's instructions and wishes; in fact, the channel through which we receive Torah is prophecy – apart from the first two of the Ten Commandments which we heard directly from Hashem, the rest of Torah comes to us through prophecy: either the prophecy of Moshe Rabbenu or of the other prophets.

What is much more difficult to understand is that as the seventh Fundamental the Rambam holds: "I believe... that the prophecy of Moshe was true, and that he was the father of all the other prophets, of those who preceded him and those who followed him." Why is this so fundamental? Why is belief in Moshe's prophecy not covered by the previous principle, that of the truth of all prophecy? Why is it so critical to believe that Moshe's level of prophecy was higher than that of any other prophet?

Even more difficult to grasp is this: the Rambam's source for these Fundamentals seems to be those transgressions listed in the Written and Oral Law for which one loses one's share in the world to come. In his *halachic* code the Rambam includes a list of transgressions for which the consequence is loss of the next world, and the elements of Torah belief mentioned there as necessary in order to generate and earn one's share in the next world are here phrased as Fundamentals of faith. In the negative: if one transgresses in one of those critical areas one has forfeited one's share in the next world (of course *teshuva*, sincere repentance as prescribed by Torah, annuls this severe consequence.) In the positive: these are the Fundamental elements of Jewish faith.

This means that when we study the Thirteen Fundamentals, we are studying those things which hold a most severe penalty for omission or transgression – these are the things which effect a connection between this world and the next for the *neshama*. Now the problem is: why is belief in the superior level of Moshe's prophecy over that of the other prophets *that* fundamental? We are saying, in effect, that one who believes deeply and perfectly in the truth of prophecy but does not acknowledge that Moshe was on a different and higher level lacks a fundamental of Torah belief which is serious enough to jeopardize his share in the next world! In fact, in *Hilchos Teshuva*, the Laws of Repentance, the Rambam states exactly that – one who denies the prophecy of Moshe, as distinct from denial of prophecy in general, has no share in the world to come. This surely needs explanation.

*   *   *

We know that Moshe was on a higher plane than other prophets: it is said that other prophets saw through an "unclear lens"; Moshe saw through a "clear lens". Just how great is the difference between these levels?

Study of this area will show us that we are dealing not with a difference in degree, but with a difference in kind. In order to understand, let us study the fascinating explanation of a section of *Chumash* which is quoted by Rabbenu Avraham, son of the Rambam, in the name of his father and grandfather and also in the name of Rav Saadia Gaon, and which he praises highly.

In *parshas Shmos*, in the Book of Exodus, we find a conversation between Hashem and Moshe. Hashem tells Moshe to go into Egypt to redeem the Jewish people and to visit retribution upon Pharaoh. Moshe answers that he cannot deliver the necessary message to Pharaoh because of his speech difficulty. Hashem answers that He will send Aharon, Moshe's brother, to be his spokesman. Until this point in the exchange, things seem to make sense; but Moshe's next comment requires explanation. We find (in *parshas Va'era*) that Moshe did not accept Hashem's offer of using Aharon as his spokesman – Moshe replies by again stating that he is handicapped in his speech. And Hashem again states that Aharon will serve as Moshe's spokesman, after which Moshe accepts. What is the meaning of this seemingly unnecessary repetition? Why does Moshe refuse at first and accept when the solution is repeated?

As always, the words themselves, understood accurately, hold the secret. At first, when Moshe objects on the basis of his speech problem, Hashem tells him to transmit the words to Aharon: "And you shall speak to him, and you shall put the words in his mouth... and he shall be to you as a mouth, and you shall be to him as an *Elokim*" (an angel).

When Moshe objects again, repeating that he cannot speak adequately, Hashem answers: "Behold I have given you to be an *"Elokim"* (again, an angel) to Pharaoh, and Aharon your brother will be your prophet." Those words, it seems, explain everything to Moshe, and he objects no further. *"V'Aharon achicha yi'hye n'vi'echa* – And Aharon your brother will be your prophet." What exactly does this mean?

*   *   *

The secret, as explained by Rav Saadia and quoted by the Rambam in his father's name, reveals a depth which is breathtaking and fully justifies his son's praise for its beauty. It is this: when Hashem first tells Moshe to go and speak His words, Moshe objects; he cannot speak well. But when Hashem informs him that Aharon will speak for him, Moshe objects again *because there is a condition in the laws of prophecy which states that a prophet must say his prophecy himself;* he is forbidden to give it over to someone else who will say it for him. Just as he must deliver his prophecy and not hide it (or evade it, as Jonah tried initially) on pain of death, so too he must say it *personally.* Moshe repeats that he cannot speak when Hashem tells him that Aharon will speak for him because he is perplexed; Hashem Himself, the One who decreed that a prophet must say his prophecy personally, is now telling him to let a spokesman say it? That is forbidden!

And Hashem's answer is illuminating beyond words: I am *not* telling you to say your prophecy over to Aharon so that he can repeat it; I am not going to make you a prophet at all; no, you will not be a prophet – *you will be the prophecy, and Aharon will be the prophet.* You will be the prophecy itself, Aharon will receive that prophecy, and what he says will be his own! *"V'Aharon achicha yi'hye n'vi'echa* – And Aharon your brother *will be your prophet"*! You will indeed and most literally be an *"Elokim",* an angel to Pharaoh; you are not the medium, you are the message.

*   *   *

Hashem was informing Moshe that his level of prophecy is of a kind that is entirely different than any other prophet's. As Rabbenu Avraham ben Ha'Rambam puts it, Hashem speaks to other prophets through an intermediate agent, through an angel; but to Moshe He speaks directly.

And that is what we need to know; the Rambam lays down as fundamental the principle that Moshe Rabbenu's prophecy transcends that of all other prophets in a most essential way. Other prophets transmit the words of the

Divine through the medium of their elevated personalities; Moshe's words are not transmitted through any medium, they are Hashem's words *themselves*. He is an entirely pure channel; his lens is so unclouded that the light itself shines here as it does there; there is absolutely no nuance of his individual personality shading the words; and when we learn the words of the Torah which he gave us we are learning Hashem's words directly.

That is what is so fundamental about this principle, and that is why it is set apart as independent. The Torah of Moshe is not a message transmitted by a prophet who has a superior command of the medium of transmission. It is simply and literally Hashem Himself speaking. And that is a fundamental of Torah faith – the knowledge that when one hears words of Torah one is hearing the Master of the Universe most directly is an essential element in our relationship with Him. That relationship is close and personal; it is a sturdy bridge between higher and lower worlds. One who ventures onto that bridge takes the first step in transforming this world into the next.

Chapter 12

Eating as Connection

If we wish to understand the duality of spirit and matter, of soul and body, we must understand the subject of food and the function of eating. We note that the Creation includes the function of eating; in fact, life depends on this function. Why is this necessary? Given the axiom that nothing in the world is superfluous, what is the essential nature of the idea of eating?

As we have attempted to understand, soul and body represent opposite polarities, and their natural state is separation. A special energy is required to keep them together, and this energy is provided by food. The function of food is to maintain the bond between body and *neshama*, to keep the *neshama* in the body. If a person does not eat, the *neshama* begins to move out, to distract itself from the body; the person becomes faint. If starvation is prolonged, unconsciousness results; a further degree of separation. And of course, if starvation is prolonged sufficiently, the separation will become permanent. One cannot live without food; in spiritual terms, the *neshama* cannot be held in the body without the connecting energy of food.

* * *

We have noted previously that the Torah uses speech as a euphemism for intimacy. It should be no surprise that the same is true of eating. "She ate... and said 'I have not sinned'" – the verse is referring to immoral intimacy. Since eating represents a function of connection between worlds, it too is a perfectly appropriate metaphor for intimacy between male and female.

At a deeper level, parallels such as these must hold true in all their aspects. If speaking and eating are closely linked at the level of their inner meaning, one can begin to understand why they are both performed by the same organ, the mouth. There are no accidents in the spiritual world: if the body is so constructed that one organ performs more than one function, it must mean that those functions are in fact only different manifestations of the same underlying theme.

Closer examination of this same idea reveals that there is another function of the mouth, which of course must also represent a facet of the same theme: kissing. The function of a kiss is intimate connection between people; it is a natural expression of affection. In truth, it is a very strange activity: we do not see it thus only due to familiarity, but it is extremely unlikely that the human mind would choose this particular act as an expression of love! If a human were asked to design a physical expression of affection, contact between people using the mouth in this way would almost certainly not enter the mind, and it would probably seem bizarre if suggested. But it is built into our behavior patterns because in essence it is perfectly appropriate. The mouth is an organ of connection, and therefore in all three of its functions we see this manifest.

*   *   *

The tools must always be appropriate for their task. If the function of food is to bond body and soul, it is critical that food appropriate for such a refined task is used. This insight is the beginning of understanding the importance of *kashrus*, the dietary laws of the Torah. The task is refined, the food must be perfect.

It is noteworthy that the Torah allows the eating of meat. Before Adam sinned, however, he was allowed only vegetarian food; it was only after the Flood that mankind entered a state in which meat eating is appropriate. Rabbi Simcha Wasserman z'tzl used to observe that in depth, this change represents a falling: to sustain life at the cost of the life of other living creatures is not ideal.

He would explain as follows: a major sin of the generation of the Flood was theft, and the corruption of that generation led to its total destruction. Before theft contaminated the human dimension only vegetarian food was permitted; after mankind chose to pervert itself with the sin of theft, meat became an integral part of our diet. The message is clear: theft means sustaining one's needs by depriving another of what is rightfully his, a person's livelihood is wrested away from someone else; the result is that man falls to a situation in which he is condemned to sustain his life by taking the life of another living creature.

The consequences of actions are always manifest in kind – *midda k'neged midda*. Mankind was saved, the annihilation of the Flood was not total; but mankind's remnant was allowed to re-populate a world in which living at the expense of the death of animals is a constant reminder of the difference in level between what exists now and what once was, between the heavy physicality of present existence and the ideal state. Our food is not *man* – manna from a transcendent world, but flesh cut from the bones of an earthly creature.

$$* \quad * \quad *$$

There are Torah sources which explain that this sentence of mankind, namely the fact that we sustain ourselves by ingesting other forms of life, is in fact its own correction. When one creature eats another, the first becomes part of the body and the life-energy of the second. The eaten becomes absorbed into, and therefore part of, the eater. When plants assimilate inorganic matter and incorporate that matter into their substance, the inorganic elements are elevated into the life-forms of the plant world. When animals eat those plants, the plants in turn are elevated to the level of the animal world. And when humans eat animals, the entire chain is brought to the level of the human.

Of course, this process is vulnerable in that the *tikkun*, or correction, made by the human depends on the spiritual level of the human who brings those elements of the inanimate, the plant and the animal to their completion: when a righteous individual is nourished by food derived from the animal world, that food is elevated immeasurably. When meat is ingested by a person who uses the nourishment of that meat to perform *mitzvos* and benefit the world, that meat has in a deep sense *become* those *mitzvos* and that benefit. The food of a person who lives correctly, spiritually, is transmuted into spirituality. There is no higher destiny for any plant or animal than to become part of the life of a spiritually developed person.

As always in the spiritual world, the converse is also true. When food is eaten by a person who makes no effort to develop beyond the level of the physical, that food is simply destroyed. In depth, it is a dismal fate for any element in the world to become part of the life of a person who achieves nothing with the nourishment derived from that element. Food which is brought to such an end has lost its opportunity to be elevated. And the ultimate degradation for an element of the non-human world is to be used by a human who performs negative and harmful acts with the nourishment derived from that element; in a sense, such a plant or animal has been transformed into negativity. This is the depth of the statements found in the teachings of the Sages to the effect that the eating of meat is not to be taken lightly.

*   *   *

The highest form of this process of elevation is found in the world of *korbanos* – sacrifices. Without a deeper level of insight the idea of sacrifices is difficult to understand: why does the Torah prescribe the sacrificing of animals? What is the purpose of giving up the life of an animal thus – the word *korban*, sacrifice, means bringing close; what exactly is the closeness achieved by a sacrifice? Why is the *Beis Hamikdash*, the Temple, a place not only of sublime music and indescribable incense, but also of animal sacrifice – this is a concept which the modern mind struggles to grasp.

The Nefesh Hachaim reveals a depth in this area based on the idea which we have been studying, the idea of connection between worlds. We have noted already that the human body is a microcosmic reflection of the Universe. Any pattern discernible in the body must have its parallel in the world. What is the function in the Universe which parallels eating in the human dimension?

The answer is this. Just as the human consists of body and soul, so too does the world in general. At the universal level, the body of the world comprises the entire physical Universe. And the soul of this immense physical structure is none other than the Divine Presence. Hashem Himself, as it were, is the *neshama* of the world.

Now just as Hashem has created the human in such a way that he must eat in order to survive, to maintain the connection between body and soul, so too has He built the world. *The world must eat in order to stay alive;* in order to maintain the soul of the world – Hashem Himself – within the body of the physical Universe, the world must eat. And the food of the world consists of the sacrifices offered in the *Beis Hamikdash.*

The Nefesh Hachaim explains this startling idea as the reason that the Torah refers to sacrifices as Hashem's "food", as it were; *"korbani lachmi* – My sacrifice, my *bread",* and many other similar references. The altar is referred to as *"shulchan gavo'a* – the *table* of the Most High."* And many of the laws of the *korbanos* reflect their connection with the idea of meals such as those eaten by humans.

Sacrifices are indeed a "bringing close", a way of holding the life energy of the Universe within its physical bounds. And the fact that we lack this practice today reflects exactly the distance manifest now between the physical and spiritual – "*Hashamayim kis'i v'ha'aretz hadom raglai* – The Heavens are My throne and the earth is My footstool," so great is the distance. The world is faint indeed. We have no open revelation of the *Shechina*, the Divine Presence, without the *Beis Hamikdash* as the pulsating core of the Universe.

We must substitute prayer for sacrifices in order to experience some of the closeness we lack; "*Un'shalma parim s'faseinu* – And we shall pay for bulls with our lips," we must use speech, that form of connection generated with our mouths, and speech in the form of prayer which is itself an expression of longing for closeness.

*   *   *

The secret of eating as connection manifests in other ways too. It is remarkable that when people eat together there is a special sense of togetherness. Why is it that a unique awareness of connection between people forms around the seemingly mundane and earthy experience of eating? The depth here is exactly the idea we have been studying – eating is intrinsically a function of connection, and when it is done in company a unique experience of human connection can be generated. In *halacha* this is reflected in the laws of *bentching* – grace after meals: when three or more eat together, a special introduction is added. And when ten or more eat together, the Divine Name is mentioned in the *mezuman*. The level of connection achieved is sufficient that the Divine Presence participates, something which takes place when ten gather for prayer – the link is clear.

*   *   *

The function of eating has two components: nourishment and pleasure. What is their common element? There is a deep relation between the experience of connection and pleasure. When disparate elements connect, bond, achieve unity, a potential for great pleasure is released. The origin of the world is Unity; the manifest world is all multiplicity, differentiation, breakdown into parts. In spiritual terms it is the particulate nature of the world, its lack of unity, which is the source of all pain. When individual parts of the world bond, when there is movement towards oneness, the result is a taste of the ecstasy of the next world. "Hashem Echad – Hashem is One", the deepest declaration of Jewish faith expresses the idea of the Oneness of the Divine. Our task in this world is to bring its parts into the harmony which reveals that supernal Unity. It is no surprise, therefore, that any bonding of separate parts into unity holds such potential for exhilaration.

Food nourishes; it provides the energy for the bond between body and *neshama*. This bond is life, and life itself is the greatest pleasure imaginable. The blessing we pronounce after experiencing the pleasure of food, "Borei n'fashos", is worded for the life energy we derive from that food, the energy which connects the opposite poles of body and *neshama* into an integrated whole which can move towards a unity with the Creator.

*   *   *

Many aspects of Jewish life are marked by meals; there are many *mitzvos* which we celebrate with a *se'udas mitzva* – a festive meal honoring the *mitzva*. It is a mistake to think that this is simply a social occasion; nothing in Torah life is superficial. The idea behind this practice is that we celebrate the togetherness with Hashem which we achieve by means of the *mitzva*, and we do so by partaking of a meal which is itself a reflection of togetherness. The root of the word *"mitzva"* contains a deep connotation of togetherness – the word *"tzavta"* means "together" in Aramaic. *Mitzvos* bring us closer to the Divine; we celebrate in kind.

Shabbos is a time of closeness with Hashem, a time when the higher world becomes tangible, and that is why the celebration of Shabbos is built around its three special meals. The Jewish table, compared to an altar even on weekdays, is further elevated on Shabbos. The day is alive with the feeling of connection between this world and the next, between the dimension of striving and the dimension of reward, and there can be no better way of expressing this connection than by meals dedicated to the sanctity of the day.

And perhaps now we can glimpse an insight into the descriptions we find of the next world as a *"se'uda"*, a festive meal. What is the meaning of this? Why describe a world in which there is no physicality in terms of that physical human activity, eating? But after studying our subject of food and eating, we can begin to perceive the inner meaning of this idea. In the world of perfect connection, of perfect bonding between the *neshamos* of the Jewish people with each other and with Hashem, the pleasure of a banquet at the altar of Hashem's table is the perfect description.

Chapter 13

Beis Hamikdash
Connector of Worlds

I.

We have seen that the mouth performs functions of connection. In the world at large these functions are located at the site of the *Beis Hamikdash*, the Temple, and are reflected in its essence. The *Beis Hamikdash* is the place of connection between the physical and spiritual worlds and the ideas of speaking, eating and kissing are all found there in their supernal roots.

Speaking – the *Shechina*, the Divine Presence, manifests in the *Beis Hamikdash*; that is the place from which the Jewish people directly draw Divine inspiration and that is where a direct conversation is conducted between the Creator and His people. The voice of the Divine was heard speaking from between the golden *k'ruvim* (angelic figures) in the *kodesh kodashim*, the Holy of Holies, in the Sanctuary. In fact, the Holy of Holies is the site of the most intimate connection between Hashem and the Jewish people; the two *k'ruvim* were locked in an embrace, reflecting the closeness of our relationship with Hashem which is most accurately perceived as the closeness between husband and wife.

Eating – we have studied the concept of eating as the means necessary for maintaining the connection between body and soul, and the parallel function of *korbanos*, sacrifices, as the means of maintaining the contact, as it were, of Hashem's Presence with the world. The place of sacrifices is the *Beis Hamikdash*.

Kissing – the *gemara* states that Heaven and earth kiss: *"heicha d'nashki ar'a v'raki'a aha'dadi* – the place where Heaven and earth kiss."* There are no empty metaphors in Torah; when the *gemara* makes this striking statement it is hinting at the nature of the connection in the most deeply appropriate terms. The *Beis Hamikdash* is the place of that connection.

At the moment of ultimate closeness with Hashem, at Sinai when the Torah was being given, the Jewish people's intense response was as if kissed by the Divine in the most immediate sense; *"Yishakeni mi'n'shikos pi'hu* – O that He would kiss me with the kisses of His mouth."* The Torah was that immortal kiss, and its immortal site of continuity is Jerusalem and the *Beis Hamikdash*: *"Ki mi'tzion te'tse Torah u'dvar Hashem mi'Yerushalayim* – For out of Zion shall come forth Torah and the word of Hashem from Jerusalem."*

*   *   *

The *Beis Hamikdash* is the place of intimate connection between Hashem and the world; Zion is that essence. There is a fascinating connection between the names "Zion" and "Yosef"; in fact, they are identical in numerical value. "Zion is called Yosef; Yosef is called Zion." What is the meaning of this association?

As we have seen previously, Yosef represents the perfectly loyal connection between man and woman; in the deeper wisdom, Yosef is referred to as the dimension of *yesod*, "Foundation", which is the concept of *bris*, covenant. The idea of the *bris* holds the dual elements of intense connection and also the exclusivity of that connection; any covenant means a mutual bonding in loyalty that supersedes bonds to others who are outside that covenant.

The correct form of the male-female relationship is represented by Yosef; that relationship which bonds man and woman, potential and actual, inner and outer. In this bond lies the secret of harmony and beauty – all beauty is built from the close juxtaposition of opposites. Great beauty in the world of sight or sound consists of the harmonized meeting of different elements; different, opposite, and yet blending into something greater than their individual identities with no clash between them.

It is not surprising that Yosef is the only male in *Chumash* who is described in terms of beauty which are usually reserved for woman. He was beautiful; his outer beauty was a reflection of his inner quality. And Jerusalem is described as the center of beauty – the *gemara* states that nine of the ten measures of beauty which came down to the world were taken by Jerusalem; in fact this means that all earthly beauty belongs in Jerusalem, the idea of one part in ten means that the rest of the world lives only on the *ma'aser*, the tithe that is bestowed by the Holy City. Yosef represents the deep and loyal bond between male and female; Jerusalem is the place of the bond between spiritual and physical, between the Divine Presence and the world, between Hashem and His people.

The parallel goes further: we have discussed the idea of eating and its link with the *Beis Hamikdash*: the idea that the world is nourished, as it were, through the Temple and its functioning. Yosef was the one who nourished the world – *"Yosef... hu ha'mashbir"*, Yosef is the provider of food for an entire world. And he provides that food with the wisdom of proper use: limits and gathers wisely when appropriate, and gives generously when appropriate.

There is much more; in fact, all the events of Yosef's life are mirrored in the history of Zion: "All the troubles that happened to Yosef happened to Zion... and the good that happened to Yosef happened to Zion," but enough has been said to indicate the direction.

II.

Jerusalem, Zion, the *Beis Hamikdash*; this is the place of the meeting of worlds. This is where the higher world flows into the lower. This is where the Creation began: the very Creation of the dimension of space began here and spread outward to form the rest of the Universe; and on this spot man was created.

This is where space begins; all of physical space derives from this place. One can consider the world as a series of concentric circles – the outermost circle is the lowest in *kedusha*, holiness, and as we move closer to the center, the *kedusha* increases. Outside of the Land of Israel, place has the characteristics of pure physicality – land is land, space is space, and there is no revelation of transcendence inherent in place. Within Israel, place is different: the Land of Israel is called *"Eretz tzvi* – the Land of the deer"; just as a deer's skin appears too small to cover the animal, the Land appears small; but just as the deer's skin does in fact suffice to cover it, so too the Land will always absorb all of its People. A mother's home is never too small to absorb all of her children.

Within the Land, there are further levels: outside of Jerusalem, the level is not as elevated as it is within the city. Within Jerusalem, the Mishna states, no-one ever complained that his lodgings were too limited or confined, despite the fact that millions of pilgrims would flood into the city during the Festivals.

Within the city itself, again, there are higher levels: inside the precincts of the Temple, space begins to manifest in a way that is clearly above the natural – the Temple courtyard was packed with people on a Festival so that the crowd was pressed together tightly, and nevertheless when the time came to prostrate themselves, there was plenty of room. "They stand crowded, and bow with expanse."

The Temple courtyard is close to the center of holiness, close to the center of Creation, close to the site of meeting between physical and spiritual; and it therefore transcends the usual rules of space and place. And the sensitive ear will hear that this transcendence is revealed to human eyes when those humans engage in that which subjugates the physical to the spiritual: it is when the people *bow* that the dimension of space opens up and reveals more of its higher Source; while standing, while in that posture that emphasizes human independence, the people are pressed together; but when they are prostrated, in that posture that manifests total annulment of independent pride and acceptance of higher Authority, they are not crowded at all – space and the world melt away.

This place, in essence, is the place where all of physicality bows to its source. Here, the proper attitude is annulment of self, prostration before the Source of the world. The first time that the place of the *Beis Hamikdash* was revealed this was made apparent: when Avraham saw the place from afar he said "And I and the lad shall go there and bow down..."

And within the Holy of Holies, the innermost chamber of the *Beis Hamikdash* in which resides the Ark of the Covenant and within which Hashem's voice is heard, the usual rules of space do not operate at all. This is the point of meeting itself; at this point space comes into existence, and it is more subject to the laws of the higher world than those of the lower: the *Aron Kodesh*, the Holy Ark, was situated entirely within the Holy of Holies despite the fact that its dimensions were greater than those of the chamber which contained it!

The dimensions of the *Aron* are clearly given in Scripture, the dimensions of the Holy of Holies are likewise written; those of the *Aron* are greater, and yet the smaller contained the greater. Nothing shrank, and nothing expanded: if the *Aron* would have contracted it would have become *posul*, invalid; and if the Holy of Holies would have expanded it too would have ceased to be valid. And yet, the smaller contained the greater.

This is the place where that which is above place manifests, and the natural laws are here being formed; while yet within this transcendent place that is not a place, the natural is not yet relevant. One of the names of the Divine is "*Hamakom* – the Place"; the world is located within Him.

Here at the hub of the wheel of the world the Divine Presence is manifest; here Hashem reveals that He, in fact, is the place of the world.

III.

There is another expression of the idea of essential connections which is to be found in the Beis Hamikdash.

The Midrash states: "There are three whose names preceded them – Yitzchak, Shlomo and Yoshiyahu." (The Midrash goes on to say that some include Yishmael in this list too – his name was certainly given before he was born; but we shall limit our study to the first three – the discerning mind will be able to extend our discussion to understand the meaning of Yishmael's inclusion here too.)

Yitzchak, Shlomo and Yoshiyahu; three who were named before they were born. In each case there was a Divine instruction regarding the name to be given, issued before birth: Yitzchak – "And you shall call his name Yitzchak"; Shlomo – "For Shlomo shall be his name"; and Yoshiyahu – "A son is (to be) born to the house of David, Yoshiyahu is (to be) his name." What do these three great Torah personalities have in common? What is the meaning of a name given before birth? And what is the connection between these ideas?

Firstly, the common factor linking these three is that they are all deeply connected with the Beis Hamikdash. More than this: each built a fundamental aspect of the Beis Hamikdash. Yitzchak Avinu built the initial manifestation of the Beis Hamikdash as the place of service to Hashem, of sacrifices, in the most powerful way: he became a korban, a sacrifice, himself. He was bound on the altar built on the site that would later become the Temple. He laid the foundation of the function of the *Beis Hamikdash*, the function of service and sacrifice, with his own being. Long before the physical structure of the *Beis Hamikdash* was built, its inner essence was being constructed.

Shlomo, King Solomon, built the second stage – the actual structure of the *Beis Hamikdash*. He built and dedicated the physical building. And he also prepared for the next stage: during the construction of the Temple, Shlomo prepared a secret underground cavern with an entrance from the Holy of Holies so that when the destruction would later take place there would be a place to hide the *Aron*, the Holy Ark, to save it from capture.

And that is what happened: when that destruction which Shlomo had foreseen occurred, the *Aron* was not present. It was not among the spoils carried off into exile by the enemy because it had previously been hidden in that underground chamber. And the one who hid it was King Yoshiyahu. The prophetess Chulda sent word to him that the Temple would be destroyed, but that he would not see the destruction – it was to occur after his death; due to his great righteousness, Yoshiyahu was to be spared living through that destruction. And he acted to avert a far deeper destruction: he moved the *Aron* into its secret hiding place.

So we note three phases in the building of the *Beis Hamikdash* – first, its essence in spirit was brought into being by Yitzchak. Its innate *kedusha*, its holiness, was brought into manifestation by that father of the Jewish people who himself was bound on the altar. Next, its physical building was done by Shlomo. And thus it must be: first, the soul or essence must be brought into existence, and only then can the material manifest. Yitzchak prepared the essence, the *neshama*, and Shlomo gave that essence expression in a physical structure.

But there is another stage too: in the process of building, essence and outer form are not enough. If that which is being built is to be part of the real world, it requires one more component – it must be given eternity. The *Beis Hamikdash* stood, it was alive with inner essence contained in an outer form, but it was to be destroyed. And in order to ensure that the destruction would be only outward, to ensure that the essence would remain alive even when the outer form lies in ruins, the heart was to be hidden. If the *Aron* is hidden beneath the site of the Temple when above it the Temple burns and collapses, the meaning is that this is not a destruction, it is only a retreating into the unrevealed.

Just as Yitzchak prepared what was needed for Shlomo to complete, Shlomo prepared what was needed for Yoshiyahu to complete. And just as Shlomo in fact completed his share in building, Yoshiyahu completed his share in hiding. That hiding was in a very deep sense a building. Yitzchak brought the heart to the world; Shlomo gave that heart a body; and Yoshiyahu secreted that same heart away so that it remains pulsating and alive in hiding while awaiting its final revelation for eternity. Yitzchak built the *neshama*, Shlomo built the body, and Yoshiyahu ensured that those two would never be permanently separated.

* * *

Now what does this have to do with names? A name is an expression of essence. In Torah, a name describes reality in the most exact way; it is in fact a non-tangible representation of that which it describes. A person's name is the most compressed expression of the essence of that person, it holds the secrets of that individual's existence and destiny. It is the core; in a sense it is the *neshama*.

The meaning of a name which is given before birth is this: when people are born into the world and then named, which is the usual order of things, the idea is that their essence begins to be manifest when they arrive in the world. They appear, and then a name must be found which is fitting. First there is the person, then there is an expression of that person's nature and purpose. But when a name is given *before* birth, when Hashem names a person before He brings that person into the world, the meaning is that such a person is already defined in essence, nature and purpose before his physical arrival. Such a person's physical nature and material life in the world are destined to be perfectly matched with his inner being if he performs his work well. After all, that inner level is clear and revealed even before he begins his task in life.

First named and then born; such a personality will be one who most perfectly fits his spiritual identity. Such people must be very close to perfection in terms of carrying out their duty in the world; they are challenged with building that which most closely reveals its spiritual source. Their essence is clear; they must reveal it in perfect loyalty to its genuine identity, and therefore their work is to reveal all inner essence in perfect reflection in the world.

* * *

And that is the nature of the *Beis Hamikdash*. As we have attempted to understand, the *Beis Hamikdash* represents the perfect meeting between inner and outer worlds. It is the demonstration of harmony between inner and outer. This is the place which most clearly represents the indivisible bond between soul and body, spirit and matter. This is the physical place and structure which is in perfect harmony with its non-physical core. This is where Hashem's Name is spoken, and this is where it is revealed.

At a deeper level, we say that Hashem and His Name are fitting: "*Shimcha na'eh l'cha, v'ata na'eh l'shimcha* – Your Name is fitting for You, and You are fitting for Your Name." This is the way it is at the Source, and in depth this is the way it must always be; the name must be fitting.

Yitzchak, Shlomo and Yoshiyahu; three who were superlative in their Divine service and who merited to reveal and eternalize the place of Divine service to the world. Yitzchak was a pure servant of Hashem, an *olah t'mimah* – a pure burnt offering. Shlomo, whose name means wholeness and completeness and who reigned for forty years of near-perfect closeness between the Jewish people and Hashem. And Yoshiyahu, about whom Scripture states: "And before him there never was a king who returned to Hashem with all his heart, with all his soul and with all his might according to the entire Torah of Moshe, and after him there never arose one like him."

Three who were close to being perfectly fitting for their names; three who revealed Hashem's Name in the place which is most fitting for Him.

Chapter 14

Predestination and Free Will

When considering the connection between higher and lower worlds, perhaps the most difficult element with which we must grapple is the paradox of Divine foreknowledge and human free will. This is a classic problem which presents itself to anyone who thinks about free will and knows that Hashem's knowledge of the future must be absolute.

The problem is as follows. It is axiomatic and a principle of Torah that Hashem is absolute and perfect in every way. Since He is above the limitations of time, He knows the future. Now if Hashem knows that a certain human action will occur, how can we say that the human being who performs that action is free: surely the person *had* to perform that action? Since it was already revealed to the Creator before it transpired, no other possibility ever really existed. The person may have *felt* that he was choosing between alternatives, but in actual fact only one possibility existed and the person was not free at all.

Logical analysis of this problem would seem to leave us with uncomfortable options: either the Creator's foreknowledge has some deficiency – He is somehow unaware of the future when it comes to human action; or we have to say that we have only an illusion of choice. The former option amounts to no less than k'fira – open denial of the Divine; the deepest axiom of all is Hashem's perfection. The latter is equally problematic – the whole Torah is based on the assumption of real human free will; for example, the doctrine of reward and punishment would be nonsense if there were no free choice: how could a person be held accountable and rewarded or punished if in fact he was not free to do other than what he did? All the Torah's commandments would be meaningless; the world of human action would be no more than an empty charade.

There are opinions which attempt to resolve this conflict by explaining that Divine foreknowledge is not causative; ir other words, knowing the outcome of an event beforehand does not mean causing it; foreknowledge is not the same as destiny. If I am able to predict what you will do tomorrow, I am in no way the *cause* of what you do; foreknowledge and predestination are two separate things. However, the Rambam, whose opinion is definitive in this matter, does not approach our problem in that way; human prediction is certainly not a cause, but Hashem's foreknowledge is entirely different – the nature of Divine foreknowledge is absolute. In other words, when Hashem knows that a certain event will transpire, unlike in the case of human prediction, it would seem that *that event must occur*, it could not possibly turn out otherwise, and that is where the conflict with free will arises.

*   *   *

What is the Torah approach to this subject? Jewish teaching in this matter is clear and explicit – despite the apparent paradox, both Divine foreknowledge and human free will exist, and both are axioms of Torah. Any denial or limitation of either Hashem's foreknowledge or of human free will is denial of a fundamental principle of Torah. Hashem is perfect, absolute and beyond time; and we have free will.

The Rambam raises our question and states that for us there is a contradiction between knowledge which precedes a particular choice and the free nature of that choice, but beyond our limited view there is no contradiction because Hashem's knowledge is not like human knowledge. He and His knowledge are one, and just as we cannot understand Hashem Himself, we cannot understand the nature of His knowledge.

In other words, there is no contradiction because the very question is invalid in the first place, just as the classic question of whether an irresistible force could move an immovable object is illogical – the question itself is meaningless. To place Hashem's knowledge within the context of time is not valid, and therefore the question does not begin. Hashem exists outside of time and all limitations, and that is beyond human understanding. We may be able to state the principle of Hashem's timelessness and absolute transcendence, we can say the words; but being finite and timebound creatures, we cannot grasp its meaning. This, in fact, is the root of those things of which we can have a *yedia* but not a *hasaga* – we can know of it, but we cannot grasp it.

Rabbi Dessler would give a *mashal* for this: imagine a map covered with a card which has a hole cut in it in such a way that one spot on the map is visible through the hole, and then the card is moved so that a second place is visible, and then a third. We perceive those places in sequence; but if the card is removed, the entire map will be seen at one glance. Similarly, we perceive past, present and future; but at a higher level, beyond the mask of the finite, all is present.

*　　*　　*

The *gemara* teaches the co-existence of free will and a higher Destiny in a striking way. The *gemara* states "*Raglo'hi d'bar inish inun arvin bei* – A person's legs are his guarantors." A person chooses his path with all the independence of human free choice, and yet his legs, those parts of the body *furthest* from consciousness, take him where he has to go according to a higher Consciousness.

The *gemara's* illustration is unforgettable and one who has studied it can never again see life as he did previously. The *gemara* tells of an event which occurred to Shlomo Hamelech, King Solomon. Of course, nothing in the Talmud is accidental; it is significant that the example chosen to illustrate our principle is one involving the wisest of men.

One day, Shlomo saw the *Mal'ach Ha'maves* – the Angel of Death. Shlomo noticed that the Angel was looking sad, so he asked the Angel the reason for his dejection. Shlomo was a true seeker after wisdom; he saw an opportunity to gain insight into the workings of the world and the higher elements behind the scenes, and he therefore questioned the Angel. The Angel answered that he had been sent to take the souls of two individuals but that he was unable to fulfill his mission.

Now Shlomo recognized the names of the two people whom the Angel of Death mentioned, and he took immediate action. In order to protect them, Shlomo had them transported instantaneously to a town called Luz, which enjoys the distinction of being that place which the Angel of Death cannot enter. Obviously, once inside Luz they would be safe.

Strangely and unexpectedly, as the two arrived at the gates of Luz, they both died. The next day, Shlomo again saw the Angel of Death, who looked elated. Shlomo asked the Angel the reason for his jubilation, and received the following chilling reply (freely translated): "Do you know why I was unable to take the lives of those two people when you saw me yesterday? The reason is that my instructions were to take them at the gates of Luz, and I was unable to get them to go there!"

What a lesson! And what a lesson for the wisest of men! Shlomo had used his free will with the intention of saving lives, perhaps the greatest use of free choice imaginable, *and he had played into the hands of a destiny waiting to happen.* His action was correct; what else should he have done? And more than this: not only did he unknowingly act in consonance with a destiny hidden from him; *he became its cause!* Of course, it turns out that even the Angel's *appearing* to Shlomo in the first place was craftily conceived; the Angel most certainly *was* able to get his victims where he needed them – by using Shlomo's free choice!

*   *   *

Where is the Torah source for this understanding of Divine foreknowledge and human free will? The Mishna states: *"Hakol tzafui, v'har'shus n'suna, u'b'tuv ha'olam nidon –* Everything is foreseen, free will is granted, and in goodness the world is judged." At first glance, this Mishna presents a problem: its first two elements seem unnecessary – as we have said, the fact that Hashem foresees everything is a first principle in Torah, it is so basic that no Mishna need state it; and similarly, the fact that humans have free will is fundamental and underlies all of Torah, it is likewise unnecessary to be stated in a Mishna. No, the Mishna is not telling us these two principles as *chiddushim*, novel ideas that we would not have known otherwise; the *chiddush* of this Mishna is that *both principles exist although they may seem to be in logical contradiction to each other*. We would have said that these two principles are mutually exclusive; this Mishna tells us the immense *chiddush* that they are both real and yet they co-exist.

As we have mentioned, the Rambam deals with this issue. But here the Rambam adds a perplexing comment: "This statement is fitting for Rabbi Akiva." In fact, this Mishna is quoted in *Pirkei Avos*, Ethics of the Fathers, without a specific author. It follows a Mishna whose author is Rabbi Akiva, but our Mishna is brought with no name; and unlike those before and after it, it does not begin with "He used to say…" What is it about this Mishna that is so particularly fitting for Rabbi Akiva that it need not mention him as its author?

The teachings of the Sages, for example as expressed in *Pirkei Avos*, are always an expression of the particular depth of the Sage who speaks out that teaching. Each of the Rabbis expresses "*marg'lei b'pumei* – the gem in his mouth"; his own particular and unique insight in Torah, his *chelek*, or portion, in Torah. He is expressing those gems of Torah which he was brought to the world to teach, and each statement in *Pirkei Avos* is the diamond which is cut and polished by the

Sage who speaks it out, his *"marg'lei b'pumei."* Each statement of a Sage is an expression of his essence, of his heart; that is why the opinions of the Sages in the Talmud are stated in the form of *"a'liba d'..."* – according to the *heart of..."* such-and-such a Sage. Let us study our Mishna and attempt to see Rabbi Akiva's uniqueness in it.

There is a third component to the Mishna – *"U'b'tuv ha'olam nidon* – And in goodness the world is judged." Judgement in goodness – what does this mean? In fact, this statement is paradoxical in the extreme. *"Din"*, judgement or justice, means Hashem's strict measure; it is exacting to a hairsbreadth. *Din* allows no leniency at all, it is total and absolute. *Din* means that sins are punished to the full with no exceptions and no forgiving. And therefore it is impossible to have "goodness" in *din*; if there is anything other than *din* mixed in with that absolute strictness it is no longer *din!* If there is the kindness or leniency of "goodness" admixed with the judgement it is not absolute, and if it is not absolute it is not *din*.

"U'b'tuv ha'olam nidon – And in goodness the world is judged"; this Mishna is teaching that the world is an impossible mixture of two opposite qualities – *din* and *rachamim*, judgement and mercy. *Rachamim* is the kindness, the goodness, that is mixed with the strictness of justice. In fact, the Midrash clearly states that the Creation contains this combination: when the world was created, *"ala b'machshava* – it arose in the mind" of the Creator "to create the world with *din*, but He saw that the world could not survive (thus); He (therefore) arose and combined with it the quality of *rachamim."*

A world built on pure *din* could not survive; such a world could not tolerate any human error at all – even the slightest of sins would result in immediate annihilation of the sinner; after all, that is what *din* means: sin is the process of conflict with the Divine, of moving in contradiction to the expressed wish of the Creator; and if the wishes of the Creator are the stuff of existence, then sin means moving out of existence. *Any* sin would mean a clash with the Creator and true existence, and any sin would mean immediate death. And therefore, in order to make human existence with its fallibility and imperfections possible, Hashem combines mercy with the justice.

This Midrash requires understanding: what is the meaning of the idea that Hashem "wanted" to create the world with pure judgement, but that He "changed His mind"? Obviously the Midrash is not suggesting that in the Divine scheme of things there are "first thoughts" and "afterthoughts". The idea here is that the world is in fact created with judgement as its base, and that judgement is not weakened or retracted. But *rachamim* is added in order that a human world can survive. And the paradox is that despite the *rachamim*, the *din* remains *din*. Note that the Midrash states that Hashem *combined* the *rachamim* with the *din*; it does *not* state that He *replaced* the *din* with *rachamim*. Somehow the original plan to create a world of *din* remains, and yet the manifest world we inhabit functions with the quality of *rachamim. And human beings cannot understand the combination.* At the root of the Creation lies this fundamental paradox: we experience the kindness of second chances, opportunities to correct mistakes, opportunities to continue living despite transgression; and yet the underlying justice is not compromised – every detail, every nuance of human action is being judged in the most exacting manner.

"U'b'tuv ha'olam nidon." The world is judged with goodness; human action is met with kindliness, mercy is extended, and yet judgement is always exact.

Here we have the root of the duality inherent in the world: a world created with *din* and *rachamim* co-existing; and derived from this duality, a world created with Divine foreknowledge and human free will co-existing.

* * *

At the deepest level, this supernal duality is expressed in the Divine Name. In Torah sources Hashem's "Name of Essence", that Name which we do not pronounce but refer to simply as "Hashem", or "the Name", is stated to mean "that which is above all attributes." In other words, this Name refers to essence, to Hashem's ineffable Being, far above any particular quality or specific attribute; that Reality in which all is One. This is unlike all the other Holy Names – each of Hashem's Names other than His Name of Essence refers to a particular Divine attribute; for example, the name *Elokim* indicates the Divine justice inherent in Hashem's interaction with His world.

However, there are Torah sources which refer to Hashem's Name of Essence as indicating His kindness, or *rachamim*. Now which is correct? Surely *rachamim* is an attribute – if so, then this Name would seem to be the Name of a particular attribute. How can the same Name indicate a specific attribute and also indicate that which is above all attributes?

The answer lies in our discussion of the highest duality. Unlike the other names which refer to particular attributes, the Name of Essence refers to *rachamim* in a far deeper sense – the meaning of the *rachamim* indicated by this Name is *that rachamim which exists together with din and yet does not negate it.* That is the highest expression of Essence which human ears can hear – that Name which expresses the highest kindliness, that kindliness which operates within the strictest justice and does not lessen that justice at all. That is the Name of Essence, and that is the Name of Oneness. The Name *Elokim* indicates a particular attribute, that of Divine justice; but the Name of Essence indicates the attribute of mercy in an entirely different way – the Unity of mercy with justice at the root of Creation; that certainly is a Name which transcends attributes and is of essence.

*   *   *

What of Rabbi Akiva? Why does the Rambam state that he is the author of our Mishna? Rabbi Akiva is the expression of *Torah she'b'al peh* – the Oral Law; *"v'kulhu aliba d'Rabbi Akiva* – and all (opinions ultimately) are according to Rabbi Akiva."* The Oral Law reveals the true nature of the themes of Creation and Torah, that which is behind the scenes. And Rabbi Akiva is the one who lived on a plane that allowed the *din* to become apparent – he was killed by the Romans in the most brutal way and his flesh sold in the marketplace. That is an end that does not reflect *rachamim.*

In fact, during that unspeakable torture in which Rabbi Akiva was teaching the ultimate service of Hashem, saying *Shma Yisrael* with his final breath as his students looked on, the angels protested. "Is this Torah and is this its reward?" they asked Hashem. Surely one as great as Rabbi Akiva deserves better? And Hashem's answer takes us back to the beginning of Creation: "Be silent! For thus it has arisen in my thought... If I hear another word of objection I shall return the world to a state of void." Difficult to translate those words *"kach ala b'machshava l'fanai..."*, but we have heard them before, at the moment of Creation when *din* was being established as the foundation of Creation, before *rachamim* was admixed. And Hashem is saying that this moment, this final moment in the life of Rabbi Akiva, is a moment of unadulterated *din*, a judgement so unmitigated by any manifestation of *rachamim* that it derives directly from the true underlying theme of the Creation, that of pure *din*.

And Hashem is saying that it cannot be understood, not even by angels. Be silent and accept; any attempt to understand is an attempt to reach a dimension which was manifest only before the Creation took its present shape; any further demands to understand will cause the world to return to that primal state of void.

Rabbi Akiva was great enough to live on the plane of *din* and to become a demonstration of that pure quality. He did not require the admixture of leniencies and excuses. Such a person takes full responsibility for the entirety of his life and conduct. Such a person reflects the ultimate level of the Creation, and such a person earns a share in the next world entirely on his own merits and efforts.

Our Mishna teaches this duality. There is Divine knowledge, there is free will, and the two co-exist. The world is based on *din*, but goodness is added to the judgement without annulling it. Despite the goodness, all is *din*. Who lived and died the contradiction between *din* and *rachamim* if not Rabbi Akiva? And who manifested that all is in fact *din* if not Rabbi Akiva? Who could be the author of our Mishna if not he?

Chapter 15

Suffering and Joy

A feature of the lower world is that it contains suffering. How do we understand its purpose? How can one be happy in the face of ever-present suffering? It is a *mitzva* to be happy – but how is this possible with so much suffering always present? Can one forget all the pain in the world and rejoice – surely that would be callous insensitivity? And how does suffering in this world form a connection with the next world?

In approaching this subject it is essential to understand the Torah view of life itself. The greatest source of happiness is the gift of life; a spiritually sensitive person does not see life as neutral, improved above or degraded below neutrality by positive or negative experiences respectively. Rather, being alive is a reason for ecstatic exultation even during the most negative experiences – life is opportunity for growth and nothing can be valued against it.

Rabbi Chaim Shmuelevitz illustrates this idea by considering the fates of Bilam and Iyov (Job). The Midrash states that Pharaoh sought the advice of certain counselors regarding the Jewish people. Bilam, that evil genius of prophecy who later sought to destroy the Jewish people by the power of his curse, advised Pharaoh to deal brutally and lethally with the Jews. Iyov, fearing for his life if he advised in favor of the Jewish people, and yet rejecting the evil option of speaking harm against them, chose to remain silent. (Yisro was also consulted – finding himself in the same dilemma as Iyov, he fled Egypt for Midian and went on to become the father-in-law of Moshe and great in his own right.)

As a result of his openly negative approach to the Jewish people, Bilam's fate was that he was later slain by the sword – a swift death. As a result of his silent refusal to commit himself, Iyov's fate was that he had to endure protracted sufferings so extreme and intense that they are proverbial. Rabbi Shmuelevitz asks the obvious question – surely the reverse would have been more appropriate? For openly evil behavior the punishment was a swift end; for equivocal behavior, which is surely far less culpable, the punishment was almost unbelievable suffering – surely a swift death is preferable to interminable suffering? But the opposite is true: the Torah is here teaching that being alive, even when the quality of that life is almost indescribably negative, is preferable to the swiftest end. Life, no matter what the quality, is of immeasurable value; life is everything.

* * *

This appreciation of life is a requirement for using it correctly. If a person lacks appreciation for the supreme value of life, it is difficult to imagine how that person can use life productively to the full; in fact, we find that the lack of proper appreciation may be a factor in causing a person to lose that gift. If it is not being used, it may be forfeited. Rabbi Shmuelevitz quotes an extreme example of this possibility.

When Yaakov Avinu met Pharaoh, the Torah records that he was asked by the Egyptian monarch "How many are the days of the years of your life?" – How old are you? Yaakov answered: "The days of the years of my sojourning are a hundred and thirty years... few and bad have been the days of the years of my life..."

Yaakov complained about his life; he was referring to the suffering he had endured – his brother Esav had tried to destroy him, Lavan had cheated him for years and also sought to destroy him, he had been parted from his beloved Yosef in the cruelest way for more than two decades, his daughter Dinah had been taken by Sh'chem; he had the weight of many sufferings on his shoulders, and he expressed this in his statement to Pharaoh.

The Sages tell us a most sobering thing: for every word of that statement of complaint to Pharaoh, Yaakov lost a year of life. He lived less than his destined years because he complained about the quality of his life – lack of appreciation of the cosmic value of life, no matter how bad the suffering inherent in that life, may lead to the gift's being withdrawn; if it is not valued, it may be denied. Hashem gives the gift of life to be used to the maximum in genuine appreciation, not cavilled at in ingratitude.

Of course, Yaakov was being judged at his supernal level: such exactitude is not for ordinary mortals; only the very greatest are held to account at such demanding standards. At Yaakov's level, the refinement of judgement is far above our level; in fact, the standards to which the greats are held surpass our understanding: if one counts the words of Yaakov's answer to Pharaoh, one does not find enough words to explain the statement of the Sages – he was to have lived as long as his father Yitzchak, but due to his answer to the Egyptian king he lived less. However, the numbers do not seem to tally: there are fewer words in his answer than the number of years he was penalized. Why? The answer is this: Yaakov was penalized not only for his own words of complaint, but also for each word of Pharaoh's question – "How many are the days...?" Now what does this mean? Why is Yaakov held responsible for the question of Pharaoh?

And the answer is this: Pharaoh asked Yaakov how old he was because he appeared old – his sufferings had taken their toll on him so that he looked old, *and that is not what is expected of Yaakov Avinu!* Had he been entirely perfect in his appreciation of the value of life his sufferings would have been as nothing in the face of the happiness of simply being alive; they would not have weighed him down so that their effects became visible, *he would not even have looked old,* and Pharaoh would not have been motivated to ask his question. And therefore Yaakov was responsible even for that question, and for being its cause he lost life.

Again, the Torah is revealing standards that defy normal human understanding, standards that apply only to the Fathers of the Jewish people. But the Torah is revealing a universal principle which applies in general at each individual's personal level. Life is invaluable; it must be appreciated and used as such.

*   *   *

One can gain at least some personal feeling of the greatness of the gift of life at rare moments. Usually, those potent moments are the ones during which life hangs in the balance – it is then that appreciation swells. Alternatively, and occasionally just as effectively, when one gains life unexpectedly one may realize its true nature and value: a patient who understands that his situation is terminal and who suddenly discovers that he is cured may respond ecstatically – he is going to live! He may be delirious with happiness and act accordingly. What has happened? Why the exhilaration? He is, after all, simply alive. But the answer is that he is alive *moments after he was not to be* – and that is the difference; being about to lose life is a very powerful generator of appreciation for that life. It is due to familiarity that we lose sight of the meaning of life; when that familiarity is shaken, we awake and savor life itself.

*   *   *

What is the connection between the sufferings of this world and the happiness of life itself? How does one generate genuine happiness even in the face of suffering?

The answer is that the very difficulties of life are the source of happiness. Let us understand this apparent paradox. The Torah concept is that this life is designed as a dimension in which one can earn the next world. The process of earning that eternal existence is all work. And work involves difficulty – work is always performed against resistance. The difficulty of the work here builds the pleasure of the reward there. In fact, the purpose of the next world is pleasure – the Derech Hashem states that that is Hashem's ultimate desire for us, to give us pleasure; and for that He has created the next world.

But we have to earn that world – and therein lies the greatest pleasure, as he explains. We are not to eat the "bread of shame", to experience pleasure as a free gift in that world would be a degrading experience; we are to build it ourselves and enjoy it as the work of our hands. Our work and our suffering here are the elements which build our happiness there.

And that is the only pathway to happiness *in this world:* to know that everything that happens here is building what will be experienced there. There is no other means of achieving any happiness in this world – any other attempt at happiness is simply escapism. Forgetfulness, drunkenness of one kind or another, can bring a temporary respite from the awareness of the world's suffering, but it is always temporary and usually highly insensitive – one who can rejoice oblivious to the ever-present suffering around him must be pathologically insensitive.

No, we are not seeking to forget that this world is full of unhappiness. Torah is not escapism, it is an objective and clear involvement with reality. And reality is full of suffering. And nevertheless a Jew can be full of joy – but that joy is not derived from forgetting; it is derived from knowing that underlying all the suffering, currents of energy are building eternity.

Nowhere in Torah do we find it stated that our goal is to be happy here. Such a goal may seem he proper pursuit of nations and cultures, but the Jew is 1ot placed in this world to be happy. The Jew is placed in this world to work and earn a happiness which is invested elsewhere. And the paradox of life is that only when work here is seen as an investment in another reality can *this world* become a source of constant joy. The *mitzva* to be happy is this exactly: to know that every tiny detail invested here, no matter what its difficulty or pain, will be paid out somewhere else in a dividend beyond description. *We are not here to be happy as a goal; we are here to be happy as a means.*

The tool needed to grasp that deeper happiness while yet in the darkness of this world is *emuna*, genuine faith; the faith that is a knowledge, a certainty, that what is planted here flourishes there. That faith must inform every action, every waking moment of life with the knowledge that the next world is alive and being built constantly; not that the next world is given because of the work done here but that *the next world is nothing other than the work done here.*

The Torah describes many curses which are the result of straying from Torah. After a lengthy and frightening description of these curses, it states that the reason for all of this punishment is *"Tachas asher lo avad'ta es Hashem Elokecha b'simcha* – Because you did not serve Hashem your G-d in joy." It would seem that joy is a primary obligation – failure to live in a state of joy is punishable by all these curses. But close attention to the words of the verse will clarify the meaning: it does not state that one must live in happiness; it states that one must *serve* in happiness. That is the emphasis: serving, working to build, that is the primary obligation; and in that serving the proper mode is joy. In fact, the verse is saying much more: the joy *results* from the serving. Real work towards Hashem is joyful; no matter how hard, and in real depth *because* it is hard, in the work lies the joy.

"Ivdu es Hashem b'simcha – Serve Hashem in joy." It does not state "Be happy"; that is not the aim. It states *"Serve Hashem in happiness"*; that is the aim. It is the serving that must be joyful, and it is the serving of Hashem that must be joyful. If a life is entirely devoted to Divine service, then that life will be entirely joyful.

This is the secret of happiness. We are never happy with total abandon; that is inappropriate in a world of suffering. A Jew should not laugh without reserve in this world, outer joy must be at least somewhat limited, but inner joy should be full. That inner joy which holds the secret of the next world must itself remain at least partially secret, until it breaks out in fullness in another place and another time: "*Az y'malei s'chok pinu* – Then our mouths shall be filled with laughter"; then it will be appropriate, then the nature of experience will be complete joy.

"For... *there is no sadness at all* in the world for one who recognizes the light of lights of the truth."

*   *   *

We feel that we are meant to be happy; we perceive happiness to be a goal, perhaps the ultimate goal. Like all human experience, these emotions derive from the world of truth. At the highest level, in the broadest sweep of things, we are meant to be happy – that is the purpose of the Creation of the human, as the Derech Hashem states. But we are to achieve that through our work; that state is the end, not the means. Our lower selves seek the end within the means, we wish to have the ultimate reward now, and without the work. But that is not the way the world is built; the pathway is to invest the work here in results there, and because the effort and pain here build joy there, we can feel some of that joy, intimations of a cosmic and eternal joy, in the work as it is being performed. That is genuine joy in this world, and that is the only joy in this world.

*   *   *

This is the connection between lower and higher worlds. The work of this world is the stuff of the next. Growing here is growing towards another dimension, and one who is sensitive can perceive that growth and the closeness to that greater dimension.

Chapter 16

Reward in This World

We have a general principle that *"S'char mitzva b'hai alma leika* – There is no reward for a *mitzva* in this world." *Mitzvos* are performed here but their reward is reserved for the next world. This world is finite, it bears finite action; the next world is infinite and it expresses the results of this-worldly actions in infinite terms. A *mitzva* here is paid out in equivalent value there, and that equivalence is infinity.

It is remarkable that almost all of the *mitzvos* consist of physical actions – only a very few are performed by thought or attitude alone. This means that the *mitzvos* function by performance of physical actions which activate effects in the spiritual realm. The action takes place here; the result occurs there. There is no reward here because the reward for a *mitzva* is the *mitzva* itself: the reward consists of the effect brought about by that *mitzva* which is experienced by the *neshama* in the next world; the change, the growth which takes place in the *neshama* of the person who performs that *mitzva* is the reward itself.

Bonding between this world and the next is effected by *mitzvos*; the body performs the *mitzva*, the *neshama* experiences the result; and since this world is the domain of the body and the next is the domain of the *neshama*, a bridge is formed between them.

*   *   *

Let us look more deeply. When the body is engaged in performing a *mitzva*, the mind should be focused appropriately – the body must perform its work in physicality while the mind transcends the physical so that the result is the translation of material into spiritual. If the intention of the one performing the *mitzva* is in fact to perform a spiritual act, an act of Divine service, then the physical action is elevated to the level of spirit, and the bond between material and spiritual has been forged. If, however, the intention is not transcendent at all, the *mitzva* lives in this world only.

The rule in the spiritual world is that all things must be paid in kind: a purely physical action can have only physical results. An action propelled into transcendence by that component of the human which is in fact transcendent, the mind, can live in the higher world. This is the reason that *kavana*, intention, is so important when performing *mitzvos*; one should be sure to intend that the action of the *mitzva* is being done *because it is a mitzva*, because Hashem has commanded this action.

To be sure, even a *mitzva* performed with inferior motives may be valid; if it meets the minimum *halachic* requirements for that *mitzva* there will be an eternal effect. The Mesillas Yesharim states that Hashem pays for even the most inferior *mitzvos* because *"Ha'kadosh Baruch Hu eino m'kape'ach s'char kol ber'ya* – The Holy One, Blessed is He, does not withhold the reward of any creature." If a person performs a *mitzva* primarily because of some ulterior motive: if one gives *tzedaka* (charity) in order to be admired, for example, there is no doubt that reward will be paid for that *mitzva* if the giver at least partially intended a *mitzva*.

But the Mesillas Yesharim's choice of words is chillingly clear: the expression *"eino m'kape'ach s'char kol ber'ya"* is taken from the reward which the Torah prescribes for dogs – the *Chumash* records that when the Jews left Egypt no dog barked, and the Torah commands that carcasses should be thrown to the dogs as a result. Even the action of an animal, which possesses no free choice at all, is duly rewarded – "Hashem does not withhold the reward of any creature." And from this we can learn that even the most inferior *mitzva*, that *mitzva* which is invested with the absolute minimum of intention, will be rewarded. But what a bite the Mesillas Yesharim puts into those words when he refers to the reward for a *mitzva* performed without spiritual intent in the same terms used for a carcass thrown to dogs for an animal action!

Conversely, even one *mitzva*, if performed truly *"l'shem shamayim* – for the sake of Heaven", has the potential to guarantee eternal existence in the next world for the one who performs it thus. *Mitzvos* are done here, but they must be invested in the next world. If a person wants real life in the world to come, his life here must be directed, dedicated, towards that world.

* * *

It is true that there may be some effect, even reward in a certain sense, of *mitzvos* in this world; but we can understand this too in the light of the principle we have been studying: things live where they are invested. When a *mitzva* benefits some aspect of this world directly, its effects may be manifest here in addition to its effects in the next world: the Mishna states that there are certain things which pay dividends in this world while the capital remains to be claimed in the next – "These are things of which a person eats the fruits in this world while the capital remains intact for the next world..."

There is a sharper application of the idea that a *mitzva* can live only where it is planted, so to speak. One of the classic answers to the ancient question of why the righteous often suffer and the wicked prosper is that the suffering of the righteous is in fact only a pruning of their imperfections in this world in order to leave them clarified in purity in the next. Even the most righteous person has performed some negative actions, and the painful effects of those actions are felt here as suffering which that righteous individual must experience in order to experience only ecstasy in the world to come.

Conversely, an evil person may experience happiness and fulfillment in this world as payment for the few *mitzvos* which even the most negative individual has performed. The ominous consequence, however, is that such an individual will have no reward in the next world because all of the merit due to that individual has been paid out here.

Now a perplexing question arises: if *mitzvos* are properly rewarded in the next world and not here, as we have learned, where is the fairness in this arrangement? Surely even the few *mitzvos* of the evil person deserve to be rewarded as *mitzvos* – in the next world? Even one *mitzva*, we have learned, is worth infinity; why then are this person's *mitzvos* different?

But that is exactly the point: an evil person, by definition, is one who has no interest in investing in a world other than this. Such a person lives here and only here. This world and all that it offers is such a person's entire investment. And we have learned that one lives only where one builds life: if an individual does not build a transcendent dimension by investing his life in transcendence, then that dimension does not exist. That person's *mitzvos* cannot be more than mere physical actions in the physical dimension; or to put it more plainly, how can reward be paid to an individual in a world in which he does not exist? Of course *mitzvos* have endless potential; but they must be performed with that in mind. When the essence of a person is shrunk to this-worldly proportions, the actions of that person shrink similarly; his actions cannot transcend his essence. When a person exchanges infinity for the finite, all of that person's expression in action must be finite; no reward can be paid in the higher world – he is simply not there.

*   *   *

Mitzva and mind, body and soul. That is the team which can effect transcendence. The ultimate marriage of physical and spiritual, within the small frame of the human, is the composite reality which reflects Hashem and His Creation. When we bond body and soul into intelligent *mitzvos*, we bond ourselves into living manifestations of the ultimate Unity.

Chapter 17

Purim and the Masked World

Some of the deepest secrets of the connection between the hidden and revealed worlds are contained in the theme of Purim. Insight into Purim yields a new dimension in understanding the ideas we have been studying, beginning with Adam's encounter with the Tree of Knowledge and sweeping through history until finally the connection between spiritual and material worlds will be openly revealed.

The word *megillah* means a scroll. The same root in Hebrew forms the word *megaleh* which means to reveal; as the scroll unfolds it reveals the hidden depths. This is remarkable because the *megillah* of Purim does not seem to contain any revelations at all. Of all the books of Scripture it would seem to reveal the least: the Divine Name is not mentioned in the entire *megillah,* and all the events within its narrative appear to be natural. There are no open miracles in the *megillah* and no prophet speaks words of prophecy. How is it that something written to conceal actually reveals? Here lies the key to revealing in one's own life areas that seem to be only darkness. We laugh on Purim because we are able to bring out joy from the hidden dimension, from that which would appear to evoke sadness. In order to understand this we shall have to go to the root of Creation.

*   *   *

R. Tzadok HaCohen reveals a dimension of insight into Purim which sheds light on all of history from the Creation until the end of time.

The *gemara* asks *"Haman min haTorah minayin* – Where is Haman's name found in the Torah?" This question needs some explanation. It is axiomatic that everything is contained in Torah; as we have seen, Torah is the source of all that exists and therefore all aspects of existence must be rooted in Torah.

Before a person or object comes into being there must be genes that code for all the details of that person or object. Those genes must be in Torah, and the deepest genes of a thing are its name. As we have noted previously, a name is an expression of essence.

The root of the word "name" in Heb·ew, *"shem"*, is also *"sham"*, "there", because "there" is the final stage of any movement or process, its *tachlis* or ultimate purpose. While there is movement towards the goal it is always "there", the focus and target of that movement. The root *"sham"* is also the basis of the word *"shamayim"* which means Heaven, the spiritual world, which is the *tachlis* of all the movement of this world, its ultimate "there". The final destination of everything in the world is its name, its original designation of essence.

The meaning of the *gemara's* search for the name of Haman in the Torah is this: what Haman represents must have its root in Torah; if we can locate his name in the Torah we will be able to grasp his essence, we will be locating his spiritual genes. We will be able to understand exactly what he is and what must flow from his personality and all his descendants and all those like him in the world. Haman, a descendant of Amalek, that nation whose single-minded aim is to destroy the Jewish people, must be located in Torah, and finding the location of his name will reveal who he is and what Amalek is.

The *gemara* finds Haman's name close to the beginning of the Torah. After Adam eats from the forbidden fruit of the Tree of Knowledge, Hashem appears in the Garden and asks him *"Hamin ha'etz...* – Did you (eat) from the tree...?" Now the word *"hamin"* is Haman. Without vowels, as the Torah is written, that word is Haman. When Hashem asks man "Did you eat from the tree...?" that question is posed with the word *"hamin* – Haman".

"Did you eat from the tree?" What has that to do with Haman? What does Haman have to do with this question that the Creator asks man? The message being conveyed here must be most fundamental because it is located at the beginning of Creation. This is the beginning of sin – what Haman is in the world must somehow be intimately connected with the root of sin itself.

Hashem is here speaking to a man who has fallen and can no longer clearly hear Him speak. Let us try to understand in depth.

This question which Hashem asks man is an expression of the distance which has come between man and his Creator as a result of man's sin. When Adam sins, he hides in the Garden. Hashem appears and asks: "Where are you?"; and then: "Did you eat...?" What is the meaning of these questions? Surely the Creator knows where Adam is and whether he has eaten without having to ask him? The answer is that He certainly knows, but man is behaving as if Hashem does not see him, and Hashem relates to man only as man relates to Him.

Adam has become so blind to reality, so confused, that he tells himself that he can hide from the One Who sees all. Only moments before he was in direct and open communication with his Creator; has he forgotten with Whom he is dealing? No; he knows Hashem, and that is precisely why he is hiding! But he has entered the world of illusion, and in his guilt and shame before the Master of the World, he somehow thinks he can hide from Him.

Adam has lost his clarity; in moving away from the Creator he has lost his vision and he has lost contact with the Source of reality. But the consequence is much more bitter: Hashem conducts Himself in the same way! Now that Adam is hiding, pathetic and ridiculous as that may be, Hashem plays by those rules that Adam has set up – "Where are you?" As if to say that the Master of the Universe cannot see him. "Did you eat...?" as if the Master of the Universe does not know.

Doubt has entered the world. Perhaps it is possible to hide. Perhaps He does not see, perhaps He does not know that man has sinned. A gap has opened between Hashem and His Creation; the gap, the chasm, of doubt. And the name of that gap, the name of that doubt, is Amalek. In fact, the numerical equivalent of the word "Amalek" is *"safek"*, doubt. The source of Amalek has entered the world; Haman has been born.

The word *"ha'min"* is no more than the question itself: in the sentence "Did you eat...?" the word *"ha'min"* is simply that part of the syntax which poses the question. That is Haman and that is Amalek: the spiritual force which is represented by Amalek is the force which distances Hashem from the world, as it were, that force which blinds human eyes to the higher truth. Amalek is the gap between Hashem and the world.

And in a tragic and irreversible way, that is what Adam wanted. He ate from the tree because he wanted to increase the scope of his own role in the world; he was not satisfied with that expression of his human free will which was represented by simply desisting from one sin. Adam felt, knew, that he was capable of far more than that, and he reasoned that if he were to bring himself and the world down into a state more distant from Hashem he would then have the opportunity to bring it back, to elevate it to its destined perfection in closeness to the Creator *of his own doing, through his own efforts.* If there is no gap, there is no room for my work. What can I personally do, achieve, if all is virtually perfect already? Let me take the risk, he reasoned, of moving things away so that I can bring them closer; surely I was put here for a significant task?

We shall examine this idea further later and attempt to identify more exactly the source of this misjudgement, but for now we note that the sin caused a distance between man and his Source. When such a distance exists, many problems begin. When there is room to move, to squeeze away from the awareness of the Divine Presence, then humans can begin to assert their own independent will in virtually unlimited ways. Yes, there has been an amplifying of human free choice, but the price is enormous – all the evil that humans can generate is now accessible, can now be loosed on the world.

*   *   *

Amalek is that nation which has attempted to destroy the Jewish people throughout history. In physical terms, Amalek is a nation of people who hate Jews with a violent and mortal hatred. But every physical phenomenon has a spiritual root, every physical phenomenon is none other than a spiritual force manifesting in the world; Amalek represents that force which would destroy the Jewish people and their destiny. And what is it that manifests as the Jewish people and their destiny in the world? What spiritual force do we represent? The Jewish people are those who must reveal Hashem's Presence in the world. That is our function. *"Atem eidai –* You are My witnesses." Witnesses testify to that which cannot be seen; if a thing is present and self-evident, witnesses are unnecessary. It is only when the thing or event cannot be directly seen that witnesses are called. Hashem's Presence is not directly seen in the world; the Jewish people are those witnesses who are charged with testifying that behind the scenes there is that Presence.

We must testify to this fact with our lives and with all of our history as a people. And Amalek is eternally dedicated to blot out that testimony at any cost. Amalek is ready to sacrifice himself to wipe out any evidence of Hashem's immanent Presence in the world, ready to do anything to maintain the gap as wide as possible. Ready to sacrifice all for that end: and the reason for this extreme behavior is because *he depends on that gap for his survival,* for his very existence; *he is that gap.* If that gap were to close, Amalek would cease to exist. Amalek is the distance between physical and spiritual, and therefore he lives in that space and will give his life to defend it.

The cosmic and eternal battle between Amalek and the Jewish people is this battle. They seek to destroy us and we must battle for our lives; in depth the meaning of this battle is that they fight Hashem and his Presence in the world, and we fight to maintain that very Presence. This is the root of all battles and of all war. Amalek means darkness and the flourishing of evil; Amalek's end means the destruction of the gap between Hashem and the world, the restoring of that closeness which reveals that all is One.

*   *   *

When the Jewish people left Egypt Amalek attacked them in the desert. They threw themselves into a suicidal attack on the Jewish people because as the Torah was about to be given, Amalek felt that they were about to be destroyed: Torah in the world is the most intense revelation of the Divine, and Amalek's essence is to prevent that revelation. Amalek knew that victory was impossible: the Jewish people were being led by Hashem Himself, they had just been miraculously delivered from Egyptian bondage – it was clear that Amalek would lose such an encounter. But they considered the attempt worthwhile because in this particular battle there is only one survivor, and they know that.

The Torah describes that meeting between Amalek and the Jewish people in these terms: *"asher kar'cha baderech*

– who happened upon you on the way." "Happened" implies coincidence, happenstance. The word *"kar'cha"* is based on the root *kar*, meaning "cold", and the idea this root conveys is threefold: the same root in Hebrew, besides meaning "cold", also generates the words *"mikreh"* – coincidence, and *"keri"* – impurity in the area of intimacy.

Cold: they cooled the Jewish people and the world's wonder at the giving of Torah. When the nations realized that Torah was about to be given to the world, there was a moment during which they considered moving towards Sinai, towards a recognition of Torah and its meaning for all of mankind. Amalek knew that if that were to happen, they would have no place in existence, and despite the suicidal nature of the attempt, they moved to prevent that universal recognition. They attacked the Jewish people; and although they were decimated and all but destroyed as a result, they achieved their aim: the world saw that it is possible to attack the Jews, they are after all human, they are at least potentially vulnerable, and the nations stepped back from the Sinai experience.

Rashi states in analogy that this is like a man who leaps into a cauldron of boiling water: he is badly burnt, *but he cools the water*. The Jewish people were flamingly devoted to Hashem and the receiving of His Torah, and that fire could have ignited the world; Amalek cooled the flames.

Coincidence: Amalek's ideology is exactly that: everything is coincidence. What may appear to be evidence for the existence of the Creator and for His direct involvement in human affairs is only coincidence; there is no proof. *Things just happen to be*, nothing is really significant. All evidence is doubtful, all proofs are far-fetched; and that is Amalek: doubt and distance.

Impurity: we represent the loyalty of the male-female relationship, and we must manifest that in our marriage with the Creator. Amalek breaks such a bond – they claim that such loyalty has no purpose, that not everything has to be brought to fruition, not everything has a purpose. On the contrary, they argue, things have no purpose; nothing is significant and there is no closeness; what is wrong with unfettered and immoral behavior? We are all *bris*, covenant; Amalek is all breach of covenant.

Just as we live to show that there is more than meets the eye, more than our own limited existence, Amalek lives to show that he is all that there is. Might is right, I am in control and I am all that matters. Amalek comes to mask reality; we strive to unmask it.

*　　*　　*

When Amalek attacked in the desert, Yehoshua led the battle against them while Moshe positioned himself above the battlefield. Moshe held his hands up, and the battle went in favor of the Jewish people. But when Moshe's hands grew heavy and sank, the tide of battle turned; Amalek began to prevail. What is the meaning of this?

While Moshe's hands were held above his head, we were able to defeat Amalek. We are the nation of *"Na'aseh v'nishma* – We shall do and (then) we shall hear (understand)."* We commit ourselves to Hashem before we understand or even attempt to assess the meaning of His Torah and where that commitment will take us. We commit ourselves because He is the Creator and He is truth; what other option could possibly be intellectually honest?

Moshe Rabbenu, that human being who contains within himself all of the Jewish people, holds his hands above his head. The hands are the organs of *asi'ah*, of doing, the head is the organ of understanding. When the hands are held higher than the head, the meaning is that practice comes before judgement, before understanding. The *na'aseh* dimension is held above the *nishma* dimension. "We shall do, and *then* we shall understand." Our actions, our real and practical commitment to You are not limited by our intellect or our ego; we shall do what is true and right regardless of our personal and vested interests. But Amalek is all ego, all vested interest. *I* am important, *I* am everything. First I judge, first I must understand; perhaps later I shall decide to act; but then again, perhaps not. It all depends on what is in it for *me*. First, my understanding, my head. Then, perhaps, my practical commitment, my hands.

And so Moshe holds his hands up. When the hands are above the head, we prevail. When the head is higher than the hands, Amalek prevails.

*   *   *

Later in history, there was another encounter with Amalek – Saul went out to battle Amalek and was charged with destroying them entirely. Let us remember that the physical battle between King Saul's forces and those of Amalek was only the lower reality; at a higher level a cosmic battle was being fought: if Saul succeeded in eliminating Amalek entirely from the world he would be eliminating the gap between the world and the Creator. The result would be Hashem's immediate Presence forever manifest, the

Messianic revelation. That battle between Saul and Amalek was a battle for high stakes indeed.

But Saul failed. When Amalek was defeated and all but eliminated, Saul spared the life of Agag, their king. In depth, Saul's action had occurred before: when Adam sinned, he was widening the gap between man and his Creator, and his motivation was to increase human free will, to allow for more human action and responsibility. At a very deep level, Saul was faced with the same options: destroy Amalek – wipe out the distance between man and his Maker and *wipe out human free choice*, or leave just some gap, just some opportunity for man's own independent achievement despite and because of that gap.

Adam had that choice and that ability to bring the world to its permanent perfection; Saul was given the opportunity to correct that original error by facing the same options and choosing correctly. But at his supernal level of greatness, far above our puny ability to judge things at such levels, he slipped. He chose to leave the gap intact, and he spared Agag.

Agag survived only one night: on the next day Shmuel, the prophet Samuel, personally executed him. But it was too late; during that night he had been with a woman and his seed was preserved in the world. She bore a child, and *a descendant of that child was Haman.*

And remarkably, there were other noteworthy descendants of Agag: Sages of the Oral Law who learned and taught Torah in Bnei Brak! What is the meaning of this dual lineage – Haman on the one hand, and Torah sages on the other? The idea is this: when Amalek lives, there is a gap between the world and the Creator, there is darkness in the world. *But because there is darkness there is the opportunity to generate light.* Amalek is the darkness, and *Torah is the light.* If the world is dark, Torah can bring light: *because* of the darkness there are Sages of the Oral Law who teach Torah, who bring Hashem into the world, as it were. The very same act which creates the gap, which allows an Agag to live and a Haman to be born creates the opportunity for Torah to light the world.

That was Adam's aim, that was at the root of his calculation to increase his free will, to widen the gap of the world. He was not without justification, he was not without a very compelling logic. Surely, it was wrong. It was not the wish of the Creator, and we are still paying the price; but we can at least glimpse the enormity of the ordeal which he faced. He disobeyed and failed; Hashem wants obedience rather than the greatest of sacrifices – as Shmuel put it: "Are offerings and sacrifices as desirable to Hashem as listening to Hashem's voice? Behold, hearing is better than a sacrifice, to listen (better) than the fat of lambs." But from that failure emerged the possibility of correction, from the downfall emerged the possibility of arising.

*   *   *

So we see that Haman, Amalek and what Purim means all begin in the Garden at the very beginning of the human experience. It is man's own action which brings Amalek into existence, and it is to be our actions which must vanquish him ultimately. On Purim we read the Megillah of Esther, that scroll which represents the hiddenness of Hashem's management of the world. The very word "Esther" means "hidden"; when the *gemara* asks "Where is Esther's name found in the Torah?" it answers: "From the verse *'Va'anochi hastir astir panai...* - And I shall surely hide My face...'"

And it is just because of this hiddenness that we can and must exert ourselves to reveal the Divine hand. When the Jews at the time of Purim were faced with events which could easily have been perceived as mere coincidence and yet chose to see that Hand within those events, that was a deep and real acceptance of Torah. At Sinai, Torah was obvious, no effort was needed to perceive the Divine, and in a sense the human role was secondary. At Purim the Divine was far from obvious, and that is why the Jewish people's acceptance of Hashem's rule then was, in the same sense, more meaningful.

Amalek's defeat at the time of Moshe and Yehoshua was great, but Haman's defeat at the time of Esther was greater. To see the light when it is overpowering is not difficult; to cause the light to shine when darkness seems overpowering is heroic. Purim is the time of masks; Hashem has gone into hiding in Jewish history, He has donned a mask. But He is not distant; if one is distant he does not need a mask to avoid being identified, the distance achieves that. No, a mask is necessary when one is very close and yet wishes to remain hidden.

The world is His mask; nature hides His Presence. But this same world, this same nature, needs only to be peeled back to reveal its Source. The ordeal is doubt; all may appear coincidental, and the Amalek ideology may be found in the culture of today – nothing has absolute meaning or value, all is accident. The mask is heavy and convincing. But that should not deter us from our function, the function of revealing the Reality behind the mask.

Chapter 18

Paradox of the Ego

I n order to understand our part in the bonding of higher and lower worlds we must go back to the beginning. Let us look more closely at the events of that first day of the world's history, when Adam found himself faced with the challenge of obedience. What exactly was the nature of that ordeal? Surely an understanding of that event will shed light on every man's direction, for Adam was, in a sense, every man. What went wrong at that electric moment? And what is the lesson in it for the rest of history, and for that part in the world's destiny that is each of our individual lives?

As we have begun to see, the ordeal was one of ego, of the desire for freedom and independence. Adam was torn between obedience and what seemed like freedom. Obedience meant performing the Creator's will, and in so doing, bonding with Him. But it also seemed to require a yielding of human independence. And this is the deepest battle: if this was the primal ordeal, it must be the source of all spiritual ordeal and it must hold the key to all human growth. This is where it began and this is where the battle is pitched. Let us understand.

*   *   *

Adam was commanded not to eat of the fruit of the Tree of Knowledge. Obedience to that command was all that was required. And if he held strong and obeyed, all would be well; the world would reach its perfection in a few short hours and be forever perfect. But Adam felt that such an arrangement lacked a significant enough part for him: what would his contribution be to that perfection? Only the passive non-action of resisting one solitary transgression? Surely he was capable of much more than that? Surely he was capable of building worlds on his own? Surely he could be tested much more severely and prove his love of his Creator much more powerfully?

Adam reasoned that if he were to eat that fruit and bring himself and the world down from their rarefied and almost perfect spirituality into heavy physicality with all the temptations and possibilities of failure which would result, *and then* hold strong, within that lower state remain true to his Creator, that would be a far greater act of service than merely desisting from one simple action of disobedience. Essentially, he wished to amplify the scope of his free will so that there would be more work to be done, and therefore more opportunity to draw close to Hashem *of his own doing.*

He sensed that there was far more scope and potential for expression of his independent free will than his given situation allowed. And he was right. And he was wrong. He was right because in truth he had enormous potential; he was close to Divine in his greatness and virtually unlimited in power. But he was wrong because in going against the Divine command he would be moving out of reality.

And this is the point to understand: in every action of human free choice which is in contradiction to the Divine command there is a powerful illusion of independence – "No-one tells *me* what to do"; there is an assertion of self which is heady in its potency. But in every action which is in contradiction to the Divine command there is a death; if Hashem is the definition of existence, then any action against Him, no matter how powerful its sense of reality, is an action out of existence.

The nature of human emotion is such that there is a resistance to doing that which is commanded from outside the self; in such obedience lies a negation of self, a negation of desire and of that deepest level of the personality which is the seat of free choice. And in such obedience there is a sense of death too – a deep level of self is being annulled, negated, slain.

*　　*　　*

Let us search further. What is the source of this ordeal of paradox? Why does the human psyche have this need for independence, for the assertion of its freedom? Why are we charged with drawing closer to the Creator and yet are built in such a way that we fear a loss of identity when we do so?

The answer is that this very independence is a Divine quality and *is the root of the neshama*, the human soul. And that is the origin of the dilemma; this ordeal is no mere superficial temptation, it is far deeper. Let us look more closely.

The Derech Hashem states the purpose of Creation. In brief overview, and with some explanation based on other sources, it is as follows: Hashem is good. Goodness necessarily implies giving; one cannot be good in isolation – benefit to that which is beyond self is a necessary element in the idea of goodness; in fact, it is the entire concept. Now in order to give, a receiver is necessary. And that is why Hashem created man. Man is that creature whose reason for existence is to receive from the Creator, and in order to give man the ultimate pleasure, the ultimate goodness, Hashem created the next world. The purpose of the next world is to be a dimension in which man can receive the greatest good possible – and that good is Hashem Himself, as it were; in the next world man is to experience a closeness to Hashem which approaches, becomes, unity with Him. Man is that creation able to receive the greatest goodness possible, Hashem Himself; and the next world is none other than that giving and receiving.

However, to receive that ultimate and inexpressible goodness and pleasure unearned, free, would not be pleasure at all. There is a concept known as *"nahama d'k'sufa – the bread of shame"*; when a person receives a free handout, that person feels shame and helpless inadequacy. One who receives charity hardly feels alive; his dependence on others is a deep source of pain. To be given the ecstasy of the closeness with the Creator undeserved, unearned, would be an eternal experience of shame, and therefore Hashem created this world. The purpose of this world is to provide the opportunity to earn the next. This world is the place in which man is free to work of his own accord, free to generate his own perfection, free to generate his existence in the next world. This world is dark and full of challenge; it is designed to provide the stage on which man operates to actualize his potential. His tools are the challenges of this world and his free choice to grapple with those challenges and overcome them.

And that is the purpose of Creation. This world to work and earn; the next world to enjoy the reward, the results of the work. Our work in this world is necessary so that we do not feel the shame of living on free gifts.

But an obvious question arises here: why did the Creator not simply create us *in such a manner that we enjoy free gifts?* Why put us through the whole ordeal of this world with all its misery and potential for failure? Why create the risk? Why not simply create a world in which we are close to Him without having earned it, without ever having experienced free will at all, and in which we enjoy that closeness intensely?

The answer to this question is a key to many things. And the answer is this: if we were created such that we found ourselves given existence and pleasure passively, never having earned them, we would not be close to Him at all. The deepest secret of man's existence is that we are created *b'tzelem Elokim* – in the image of the Divine; at its root this means that just as He is a Creator, man is a creator; just as Hashem is free, man is free. Just as Hashem is free to create and destroy worlds if He so desires, man is free to create and destroy worlds. Really free; being created in the Divine image means modelled on the Divine in the most real way. And we are free to create ourselves: we have the capacity to develop the raw material of our personalities and our lives towards perfection.

If we were passive creatures without free will, we would be as opposite to the Divine as it is possible to be. If we were to exist eternally without having generated that eternity we would be near-lifeless puppets entirely unlike our Creator. We would be His opposites: He would be the Creator, we the creations. He would be the controller, we the controlled. He would be the giver, we the takers. And that would place us infinitely far from Him. The secret of the unity of Creation requires that Hashem and the creature whom He has created in His image are in fact reflections. We reflect Him; we are deeply similar to Him. And therein lies our potential for closeness to Him. At root, the degradation of the "bread of shame" is the feeling of distance from Hashem.

*   *   *

So we learn that human independence has its origin in the Divine image. Building worlds is our business; we reflect the Divine most closely when we build our world. *And that is why Adam experienced the most difficult of ordeals:* to obey meant to sacrifice, to relinquish his independence, to negate his freedom. The very deepest level of his being cried out to assert that freedom, to maximize his free choice. After all, that is acting in parallel with the Divine, that is expressing the Divine image. His ordeal was agonizing not because his lower self, his crude physicality, was lusting to be satisfied; he had none of that crude physicality. No; what was longing for expression was precisely his higher self, his Divinely modelled freedom to choose independently, his deepest essence.

And that was confusing. He was certain that he had been created to express his freedom, not suppress it. Obedience to one simple command was surely not a full expression of his freedom to choose? Where would all his freedom be if he merely obeyed and watched the world perfect itself without his own massive and heroic effort? Surely Hashem must mean something else in His command – perhaps He means only that eating will be so dangerous that He does not require me to do it; perhaps His command is in fact only a warning; let me show Him that I am ready for that danger, I am ready to take on all of life, and death too, to show who I am in reality.

The positive side: readiness to serve, readiness to sacrifice, readiness to enter danger, even to die – after all, Hashem had told him that he would die if he ate. And the justification: what is my free will for if not to be used, asserted?

But the negative side: I must be independent; I must act; I must be the builder of my own life; I must not sacrifice my independent sense of self in a melting into something greater than myself. I will do *anything* to remain myself; I shall not yield my will.

And here is the paradox. While man asserts his independence, he is nothing, merely a small bundle of protoplasm asserting the scope of his smallness. But when he annuls his independence, negates his ego, he melts into the reality of a greater Existence and *thereby achieves real existence*. And not merely existence as an unidentifiable part of a greater whole: no, existence as a great human being. Moshe was perhaps the greatest human who ever lived, and the Torah clearly indicates the reason: he was the humblest who ever lived. He was able to completely annul his independence and become totally attached to the Creator; and the result was not that he disappeared, but that he became the most famous individual who ever lived.

So what is the true purpose of the free will we are given? The answer is that its highest use is to give it up, to yield it to Hashem. But here lies the secret: the act of yielding the freedom to choose *is the greatest act of free choice possible.* That act is not a sacrifice of will; in depth it is the highest assertion of will. That is the challenge Adam was given: use your will to want what I want; kill not your freedom to choose but that part of it that seeks to make you separate from Me. Use your will; use it to give it to Me; in that way we shall become One.

Do not seek heroics; do not seek to prove what you can do. Simply obey; anything else is no more than assertion of ego. Such assertion of self feels good while it lasts, deeply good because it is an expression of human essence; but in truth it is illusion. Do not choose to be free; choose instead to be obliged – bondage to Me in true obligation is the real freedom.

*   *   *

In the work of sacrificing the ego, it is easy to be misdirected – destroying the negative aspects of the ego, the vested interests, does not mean destroying the will. One who has conquered the ego should not be an unmotivated robot – quite the contrary; one should be burning with motivation. The dedication of the faculty of *bechira*, free will, to the Creator does not mean sacrificing will; the mistake which can be made here is to destroy all motivation and become an empty, emotionless vacuum of a personality. That is not what is required. The spiritual path here is to *sharpen* the will, to hone to a razor's edge the drive of the will, to fan the flames of raw motivation and desire into a blaze – and *fully active and flamingly alive,* to give them to Hashem.

A true servant is not an empty shell of a human from whom all content has been drained, a mechanical and bland being who lacks all will and interest. Exactly the opposite: a true and valuable servant is one who burns with motivation, whose will is powerful and unshakable, but whose will is poised constantly to carry out the wishes of the master, not the personal vested interests of the servant. He has made his master's will his will, he acts as passionately for his master as he possibly could for himself because there is no difference between his master's desires and his own.

*   *   *

When the Jewish people accepted the Torah, they said *"Na'aseh v'nishma* – We shall do, and we shall hear."* They committed themselves to obey before they knew what that obligation would mean. Many depths are contained here, but relevant to our discussion is this: Torah is all obligation, as we have seen. The Jewish people knew that. And they knew that Torah must be received and fulfilled as obligation. They obligated themselves to Hashem without knowing the details because that is the true nature of such obligation – it is my commitment to You that matters, not my judgement of whether or not I can fulfill this or that detail. And so they took on Torah as pure obligation. *But they chose that obligation;* they chose to be forever bonded and obliged.

And that is why at Sinai the Torah was forced on us! At Sinai Hashem forced His Torah on us with no alternative. But the Jewish people had already accepted Torah – why was it necessary to use force at the actual giving? The idea is that what had been accepted was *Torah as obligation* – not Torah as voluntary observance. The Jewish people had chosen to give away their free will forever in this matter, chosen to become obliged, used their freedom to become bonded. And that was a step in the direction of correcting the original problem of man; at Sinai the Jewish people stood at the level of Adam before his fall.

That is the only way to correct that original problem. That problem remains our constant ordeal, and our path is the path of Torah; Torah as obligation, Torah as the pathway of using free will to elevate that will to a higher plane. That is the pathway to the bonding of worlds.

Glossary

Avraham Avinu: our father Abraham

Beis Hamikdash: the Temple
beis midrash: study hall of yeshiva
Bereishis: Genesis
bitachon: trust
bracha: blessing
bris: covenant; circumcision

Chazon Ish: Rabbi Avraham Yeshia Karelitz, of Lithuania and
    later Bnei Brak (d.1953)
Chumash: the Five Books of Moses

derech eretz: correct behavior reflecting good character
daven: pray
Derech Hashem: work on Judaism by Rabbi Moshe Chaim
    Luzzatto (1707 – 1746)
Devarim: Deuteronomy
din: strict justice

emes: truth
emuna: faith
Eretz Yisrael: the Land of Israel

gemara: Talmud, the Oral Law

Ha'Kadosh Baruch Hu: the Holy One, Blessed is He
halacha: Torah law
Hashem: lit. "the Name"; G-d
hashgacha: Providence
hishtadlus: natural effort

kashrus, laws of; laws of permitted and forbidden foods
kedusha: holiness

l'shem shamayim: for the sake of Heaven
lishma: lit. "for its own sake", for the sake of Heaven

mashal: analogy, parable
Mashiach: Messiah
megilla: scroll; the Book of Esther
Mesillas Yesharim: classic *mussar* (character-building) work
      by Rabbi Moshe Chaim Luzzatto; (Italy, 1707 – 1746)
mezuman: special form of grace after meals when three or
      more eat together
midda k'neged midda: measure for measure
Midrash: Torah sources which delve deeper than the plain
      understanding
Mishna: the definitive statements of the Oral Law
mitzva, mitzvos: commandment, commandments
Moshe Rabbenu: Our teacher Moses
mussar: the study and practice of Torah character-building

nachash: serpent
Nefesh Hachaim: classic work by Rabbi Chaim of Volozhin
      (1749 – 1821), disciple of the Vilna Gaon

neshama: soul

parsha: Torah portion
pasuk, p'sukim: Scriptural verses
Pirkei Avos: Ethics of the Fathers; Mishna of ethical teachings

Rabbi Dessler: Rabbi Eliyahu Eliezer Dessler (1891 – 1954) of
    Russia, London and Ponovez Yeshiva in Bnei Brak
Rabbi Simcha Zissel Ziv: Leading exponent of *mussar,*
    disciple of Rabbi Yisrael Salanter; the "Alter of
    Kelm"
Rabbi Tzadok Ha'Cohen: Rabbi Tzadok Ha'Cohen
    Rabinowitz (1823 – 1900); Lublin
Rabbi Yerucham Levovitz: *mashgiach* ("spiritual supervisor")
    of the Mir Yeshiva in the past generation
Rabbi Yosef Karo: Author of the Shulchan Aruch (Code of
    Jewish Law); Tzfas, 1500's
rachamim: kindness
Rama: Rabbi Moshe Isserles; Cracow; contemporary of Rabbi
    Yosef Karo; his glosses to the Shulchan Aruch are
    definitive for Ashkenazi Jewry
Rambam: Rabbi Moshe ben Maimon (1135 – 1204);
    Maimonides
Rav Saadia Gaon: Babylonian Sage of the Geonic period;
    (882 – 942)
Rebbe: Rabbi, teacher
Rishonim: 10th – 15th century Talmudic authorities

sh'lita: abbrev. for "may he merit long and good days"
Shabbos: Sabbath
Shita Mekubetzes: classic compendium of Talmudic
    commentaries of *Rishonim*

shiur, shiurim: lesson (or lecture), lessons
"Shma Yisrael...": statement of Hashem's unity
Shmos: Exodus
Shulchan Aruch: Code of Jewish Law; authored by Rabbi
    Yosef Karo
simcha: joy

tachlis: purpose
talmid, talmidim: student, students
Talmud: the Oral Law
Tanach: Scripture
tzaddik, tzaddikim: righteous person (sing., plural)
tznius: modesty

Vilna Gaon: Rabbi Eliyahu ben Shlomo Zalman of Vilna
    (1720 – 1797)

Yaakov Avinu: our father Jacob
yeshiva, yeshivos: academy of Torah learning (sing., plural)
Yitzchak Avinu: our father Isaac

z'tzl: zecher tzaddik livracha - of blessed memory

References

Chapter 1 Torah – the Cause of Reality
King Yannai and the Oral Law: Kiddushin 66a
R. Yehoshua, R. Eliezer, *"lo ba'shamayim hi"*: B. Metzia 59b
T. Yerushalmi concerning bodily change: T. Yerushalmi
    Kesubos 1, 2; and Nedarim 6, 8
Nechunia *chofer shichin*, R. Chanina ben Dosa:
    Yevamos 121b, B. Kama 50a; and Shita Mekubetzes;
    also T. Yerushalmi Shekalim 5, 1

Chapter 2 The Mask of Nature
R. Dessler *z'tzl*
R. Chanina, vinegar burning: Taanis 25a

Chapter 3 Behind the Mask
R. Dessler *z'tzl*
Expl. of first level: R. Simcha Zissel *z'tzl*
Elisha reviving boy: Kings II, ch.4
Elisha, Shunamis: Kings II, ch.4
Pharaoh's daughter: Shmos 2, 5; and Rashi there
King David, King Asa, King Yehoshaphat, King Chizkiyahu:
    Eicha Rabba 4
Man with milk: Shabbos 53b

Chapter 4 The World Parallels its Root
Chen makom al yosh'vav: Sotah 47a

Chapter 5 Levels of Order
R. Dessler *z'tzl*

Chapter 6 Hidden World, Revealed World
Ein ha'bracha m'tzuya...: Taanis 8b; Bava Metzia 42a
Nakva s'charcha alai v'etena: Bereishis 30, 28

Chapter 7 Words Real and Unreal
Fire and straw; *V'haya beis Yaakov esh:* Ovadia 1, 18
"I have much" Bereishis 33, 9
"For I have everything" Bereishis 33, 11

Chapter 8 The World of Obligation
"Face of the generation like face of the dog": Sotah 49b
Expl. by R. Elchanan Wasserman, *Ikvesa d'Meshicha*
In a democracy...: R. Shimshon Raphael Hirsch, Collected
Writings Vol. I, p. 341: "In Israel the law did not grow
out of the nation; the nation grew out of the law..."
Also on Devarim 17, 14

Chapter 9 Intimacy and Morality
Hashem "plays" with the Torah: Shabbos 89a
V'hinei Yitzchak m'tzachek...: Bereishis 26, 8

Chapter 10 Speech, Prophecy and Wasting Words
Bris ha'lashon: Sefer Yetzira Ch. 6, mishna 7
Hanefesh asher usu...: Bereishis 12, 5
"They saw her speaking...": Mishna, Kesubos ch.1
Niv s'fasayim: Isaiah 57, 19
"So shall be My word...": Isaiah 55, 11
Kaf ha'kela...: Iggeres Ha'Gra

Chapter 11 Clouded Lens, Clear Lens
Rabbenu Avraham ben HaRambam on Chumash; Sh'mos

Chapter 12 Eating as Connection
"She ate… and said": Mishle 30, 20
Ha'shamayim kis'i: Isaiah 66, 1
U'nshalma parim s'faseinu: Hoshea 14, 3

Chapter 13 *Beis Hamikdash* - Connector of Worlds
"Heicha d'nashki ar'a v'raki'a…: Bava Basra 74a
Ten measures of beauty…: Kiddushin 49b
Yosef… hu ha'mashbir: Bereishis 42, 6
All that happened to Yosef happened to Zion…: Tanchuma,
    Vayigash 10
Eretz tzvi: Rosh Hashana 13a based on Daniel 11, 41
They stand crowded…: Pirkei Avos 5, 5
Avraham - "And I… shall bow down": Bereishis 22, 5
Yitzchak, Shlomo and Yoshiyahu…: Bereishis Rabba 45
Shimcha na'eh l'cha…: Machzor
"And… there never was a king…(Yoshiyahu)": Kings II 23, 25

Chapter 14 Predestination and Free Will
Rambam, Hilchos Teshuva 5 (and Raavad there)
Raglohi d'bar inish…: Succah 53a; with Rashi
Hakol tzafui…: Pirkei Avos 3, 15 with Rambam's commentary
Ala b'machshava: Rashi on Bereishis 1, 1 (re Creation)
Ala b'machshava l'fanai: Menachos 29b (re Rabbi Akiva)
V'kulhu aliba d'Rabbi Akiva: Sanhedrin 86a

Chapter 15 Suffering and Joy
R. Chaim Shmuelevitz z'tzl; Sichos Mussar 5731, *ma'amar* 3
Midrash on Yisro, Bilam, Iyov: Shmos Rabba 1, 9
"Because you did not serve… in joy": Dvarim 28, 47
Ivdu es Hashhem b'simcha: Tehillim 100, 2
Az y'malei s'chok pinu: Tehillim 126, 2
"For… there is no sadness at all" Chazon Ish; letters, 36